Judicial Scrutiny of the Electoral Process in a Developing Democratic State

Judicial Scrutiny of the Electoral Process in a Developing Democratic State

Editors
E L Kwa, A Gelu and W Golman

UBSPD
UBS Publishers' Distributors Pvt. Ltd.

First Published 2003

Published by School of Law
University of Papua New Guinea
PO Box 317
University NCD
Papua New Guinea

Camera-Ready-Copy (CRC) production by Lois Stanley
School of Law Publication Unit
University of Papua New Guinea
PO Box 317
University PO 134
Papua New Guinea
E-mail: Law.Publications@upng.ac.pg
Fax: 3267 187
Phone: 3267 516

ISBN 9980-84-508-2
National Library, Waigani

In association with

UBS Publishers' Distributors Pvt. Ltd.
5 Ansari Road, New Delhi-110 002 (India)

Cover Design: Kalakriti Studio
Printed at: Nutech Photolithographers, Delhi

FOREWORD

The electoral process is an important component of the democratic process. In democratic countries the process provides an opportunity for the people to give their verdict on the performance of their elected leaders and their government. In Papua New Guinea (PNG) the electoral process is regulated by the *Constitution* and a series of Organic Laws. These Organic Laws are: the *Organic Law on Provincial Boundaries*; the *Organic Law on the National and Local-level Government Elections* (OLNLGE) and the *Organic Law on the Integrity of Political Parties and Candidates* (OLIPPC).

The *Organic Law on Provincial Boundaries* defines the political and administrative boundaries of the 19 provinces of the country. The OLNGLE is the principal legislation governing the conduct of elections in the country for the national Parliament and the local-level governments. The same Organic Law also establishes the Electoral Commission as an independent institution of the state free from all direction and control by any person. Also the OLIPPC regulates the conduct of political parties and candidates before and after an election. The roles and implications of these Organic Laws are discussed in some detail by various authors in the text.

This text is a compilation of papers presented at the Papua New Guinea National Legal Convention held at the Gateway Hotel in Port Moresby, Papua New Guinea. The theme of the conference was 'Judicial Review of Election Petitions'. This theme was chosen because of the increasing number of election petitions that went before the courts after the 1997 National Election. The Papua New Guinea National Legal Convention, which comprises representatives from the Judiciary, the Papua New Guinea Law Society, the UPNG Law School, the Legal Training Institute and the Department of Attorney General, agreed in early 2001 to organize this conference. It was organised to cover the theme in anticipation of the forthcoming National Elections in 2002.

The principal reason for the conference was to share experiences and canvas ideas to streamline the election review process in preparation for the 2002 National Elections. The Committee therefore, invited a number of prominent legal practitioners, academics and judges to present papers covering the various aspects of the election petition review. Chapters 1 and 2 by Alphonse Gelu and Eric Kwa and Wilfred Golman, respectively, have been added to this text to provide background information on the electoral process and the institution of the election petition process both at the National Court and the District Courts. These two chapters complete the flow of discussions contained in this text. I am happy that the range of chapters in this text reflects this array of experiences and ideas.

Last year, after the conference, the three editors requested the Committee for permission and funding to publish this legal text. The Committee responded positively to the request because of the importance of the theme of the conference and the need to make the proceedings of the conference widely accessible to the public and also to provide a legal text on elections in Papua New Guinea.

Two of the editors, Mr. Eric Kwa and Mr. Alphonse Gelu, are PhD scholars from the University of Auckland, New Zealand, and the third, Mr. Wilfred Golman, is a Lecturer at the UPNG Law School and also a member of the Committee. As the Chairman of the Papua New Guinea

National Legal Convention Committee, I wish to commend and thank the three editors for taking on this task and completing this text in time for the next flurry of election petitions that will find their way into the courts after this year's National Election. The text will prove very valuable in this context.

There are many important issues that have been raised by the various authors which provide useful tools for the improvement of the election review process. The text will, no doubt, provide useful guidance and source material to both the legal practitioners and the election petition disputants, and also the wider legal community and the general public.

May 2002 **Justice Gibbs Salika**

Judge
National and Supreme Courts
Papua New Guinea

Chairman
National Legal Convention Committee
Port Moresby
Papua New Guinea

ACKNOWLEDGEMENTS

The idea of this text was born in Auckland, New Zealand, in September 2001. It was at one of the usual meeting between Alphonse Gelu and Eric Kwa that the idea was mooted. A quick email to Wilfred Golman at the University of Papua New Guinea (UPNG) Law School interested him and he agreed to work together with Gelu and Kwa on the project.

The idea was influenced by the absence of a legal text on elections in Papua New Guinea. It also came as a result of the enactment of the *Organic Law on National and Local-level Government Elections, 1997* (OLNLGE) and the *Organic Law on the Integrity of Political Parties and Candidates, 2001* (OLIPPC). The OLNLGE was first applied in the 1997 National Elections and the OLIPPC is being applied for the first time in this year's National Elections; it is therefore timely that the impact of these new laws on the electoral process is recorded to indicate the direction the law is taking.

We would like to firstly thank the Papua New Guinea National Legal Convention Committee chaired by Justice Gibbs Salika for granting us permission and funding to publish this text. Our special thank you also goes to the organizations that comprise the Committee namely: the Judiciary, the PNG Law Society, Law School—UPNG and the Department of Attorney General. We also extend our special thanks to AusAid through the PNG Legal Capacity Building Project for its support in strengthening and building legal capacity in the law and justice sector.

We also extend our thanks to Ms Lois Stanley for typesetting the text, and the UPNG Law School Publication Unit, and especially the Executive Dean of the School, Professor Lawrence Kalinoe, for allowing us to use the facilities of the Unit to put together this text. Thanks also to Sakarepe Kamene from the Language and Communication Strand of the School of Humanities and Social Science of UPNG for proof-reading the text.

Our wives Enaha Peri Kwa, Ruth Kokiva Gelu and Jane Golman, and our children had to endure long hours of neglect while we edited the papers. We thank them for their unending support.

Eric L Kwa
Auckland

Alphonse Gelu
Auckland

Wilfred Golman
Port Moresby

Introduction

Kwa, E L, Gelu, A and Golman, W

The concept of election is an important attribute of the democratic process. Its application varies from one country to another. As Gelu points out in Chapter 1, even elections which are meant to be fair and free can be convoluted and abused in democratic countries. In Papua New Guinea (PNG) elections are guaranteed by the *Constitution* of PNG. In fact participating freely in an election is a qualified right of every citizen. The judiciary which is empowered by the *Constitution*[1] to protect and promote this and other constitutional rights is very overzealous of this responsibility.[2] Where it discovers that there is a breach of this right, the court will easily declare the election process invalid. Also if there are attempts to curtail the citizens' right to participate freely in an election, the courts will quickly rule against the initiative.[3]

The rights of the citizens to stand for public office and vote in elections is stipulated by section 50 which must be read in conjunction with sections 103, 125 and 126 of the *Constitution*. These constitutional provisions are complemented and expanded by the *Organic Law on National and Local-level Government Elections* 1997 (OLNLGE). This Organic Law repealed and replaced the *Organic Law on National Elections* (OLNE). The new Organic Law was first applied in the 1997 National Elections. In response to the new law, the judiciary organized a workshop in 1997 just before the elections and with the assistance of the legal fraternity adopted the *Practice*

Direction Relating to Election Petitions. This document applied only to the National Court sitting as the Court of Disputed Returns. After the 1997 Elections and in the ensuing years, it was realized that there is still a lot that needed to be done to standardize the law and practice relating to election petitions and especially review of election petitions by the Supreme Court.

In this light the Papua New Guinea National Legal Convention Committee which comprises representatives of the main stakeholders in the legal fraternity adopted as the theme for the 2001 Conference "Judicial Review of Election Petitions." The principal aim of the conference was to provide a forum for these stakeholders to discuss their experiences under the OLNLGE and propose ways of fashioning the law on election petitions. The collection of papers in this text set out the experiences and observations of lawyers, judges, academics and constitutional office holders about the new Organic Law. These papers show the way the law is evolving and highlight some very serious gaps in the law that require immediate attention.

There is general consensus that apart from the provisions relating to Local-level Government Elections, the new Organic Law does not deviate much from the OLNE. Kwa and Golman provide a detailed analysis of the "shift in the law" in Chapter 2 and conclude that in fact the passage of the OLNLGE has purportedly "opened up new horizons", which have been exploited extensively by election petitioners and their lawyers. These purported opportunities arose primarily because of the absence of appropriate rules and procedure for managing election petitions in the National Court and the Supreme Court. The absence of relevant mechanisms and the impact these had on the electoral review process especially in the Supreme Court are discussed by the Chief Justice, Sir Arnold Amet in Chapter 3, private lawyer, Camillus Narakobi in Chapter 5, legal commentator, Kwa in Chapter

6 and the Registrar of the National and Supreme Courts, Lawerence Newell in Chapter 7. The three main areas of concern which have been identified and highlighted by the authors are:

- Increase in judicial review of election petitions;
- Delay in prosecuting petitions; and
- Legal Costs.

These issues have been dealt with by the Chief Justice in Chapter 3, Sheehan, Narokobi and Kwa in Chapters 4, 5 and 6, respectively. The authors agree generally that these issues have to be resolved quickly before the elections this year. This can be done through concise and stringent practice directions. Amet CJ, however, proposes the elimination of preliminary applications and a separate Supreme Court bench tasked to deal specifically with election petition reviews. If the Chief Justice's second proposal is accepted, this will reduce the problem of inconsistencies in decisions and also speed up the review process. Newell argues in Chapter 7 that some of these issues can be easily overcome with the adoption of better and workable case management practices.

The Chief Justice shows in Chapter 3 that 25 election petitions went for review after the 1997 Elections. This is an increase of 17 petitions after the 1992 Elections. He provides concrete statistics that show that less than 10 per cent of the election petitions actually succeed. This is a very strong indictment against election petitions. The increase in election petition reviews in the Supreme Court can be attributed to two main factors. First, the propensity of lawyers rushing to the Supreme Court to invoke its powers under section 155(2)(b) of the *Constitution*. This initiative is taken, in the majority of the cases, during the preliminary stages of the hearing, usually against interlocutory orders. This approach is criticized by Narakobi in Chapter 5. He argues that if lawyers are prudent they can easily bring an election review to an end quickly by linking section 220 of the OLNLGE to sections 10 and 12 of the *Constitution*.

Sheehan, who is also a member of the judiciary, raises the same concern in Chapter 4. Sheehan actually argues that the courts have misapplied the principles of s 155(2)(b) laid down in *Avia Aihi v The State* [1981] PNGLR 81 and proposes that the Supreme Court should adopt a narrow interpretation of *Avia Aihi* to prevent the abuse of the process described by the Supreme Court in *Parry Zeipi v Gabia Gagarimabu and Electoral Commission* (SCR 5 of 1998)[4].

Second, the absence of appropriate Supreme Court rules on election reviews has meant that all the parties (election petition disputants, judges and lawyers) involved in the review process have had to grapple with ad hoc rules to prosecute the cases. This has created two obvious problems: (1) the lack of consistency in judicial precedents has caused the law to be (using the words of Narakobi) "in a state of flush"; and (2) the entertainment of unnecessary judicial applications which stretched the resources of the judiciary to the limit.

At the conclusion of the Conference in 2001, the participants agreed to set up a working committee to review the 1997 *Practice Directions on Election Petitions* and to formulate an appropriate set of Supreme Court rules on election reviews. It is pleasing to note that before going to the press the committee[5] has now developed two sets of rules which will be applied after the 2002 Elections. These are: (1) *National Court Election Petition Rules*, and (2) *Supreme Court Election Petition Review Rules*. There are two general observations about the *National Court Election Petition Rules*. First, the practice directions have now been converted into rules essentially to give certainty and impose greater legal responsibility on the parties to comply. Second, filing fees have now been increased from K50.00 to K250.00.

In relation to the *Supreme Court Election Petition Review Rules*, four main observations can be made about the rules. First, before an application for judicial review can be entertained by the Supreme Court, it must first satisfy leave requirements under the rules. These rules have been adopted from the *National Court Rules* and modified accordingly. This innovation will hopefully prevent the institution of frivolous, vexatious and abusive election reviews thus, reducing the number of election reviews generally. Second, where leave is granted the successful party is required to act expeditiously to resolve the dispute before the Supreme Court. The main strategy employed here is time limitations and the imposition of a K5,000.00 fee for security for costs to be paid to the court after leave is granted and before the review is prosecuted. Third, the review of interlocutory decisions of the National Court by the Supreme Court are now banned under the rules. Fourth, although the rules are new, it is quite lengthy as it contains 28 clauses.

Hopefully, these two sets of rules will reduce the number of election petitions going before the National Court and the Supreme Court. These two sets of rules are annexed to the text.

In relation to the issue of delay, especially in the Supreme Court the new rules have set stringent time limits which must be complied with to avoid the matter being struck out. Another issue which became very controversial is the use of the "Slip Rule". This is not a new strategy. This strategy is available again under section 155(2)(b) of the *Constitution*. The law has been settled by the Supreme Court in the case of *Wallbank and Minife v The Independent State of Papua New Guinea* [1994] PNGLR 78. In that case the court ruled that in civil cases generally, the court could use its discretionary power to correct a mistake in its first decision. The court further ruled that this power "should only be exercised where there has been a mistake which could be said to be a little short of extraordinary and affects an unsuccessful party".

The issue then is can the Supreme Court review its own decision? If the answer is affirmative, then what criteria should the court apply to allow the second or third review? This issue was dealt with in relation to the 1997 election petition reviews in several cases including the case of *Sir Julius Chan v Ephraim Apelis and Electoral Commission* (1999) SC 591; *Korak Yasona v Castan Maibawa and Electoral Commission* (1998) SC 127; *Takai Tapi v Daniel Kapi and Electoral Commission* (1998) SC 570; *Application to Re-open a Case by Peti Lafanama* (SC 16 of 1998) and *David Lambu v Peter Ipatas and Ors (No 3)* (SC 601). Generally, the Supreme Court has adopted the principles laid down by the Supreme Court in the *Wallbank* case.

In *Korak Yasona v Castan Maibawa and Electoral Commission* (SCR 127 of 1998) the court held that "section 155(2)(a) of the *Constitution* prohibits any further or other right of appeal and further section 155(4) prohibits any further or other right of review by a differently constituted court". If a party fails to argue a point of law supported by credible and compelling evidence in the first review he or she cannot raise these arguments in the second review. Thus, in *Takai Kapi v Daniel Kapi and Electoral Commission* (1998) SC 570, the court had to reluctantly reject Takai Kapi's application although it conceded that had the arguments been raised in the first review he could have won the election. Takai Kapi was still not satisfied with the decision and requested for another review (third attempt) in *Takai Kapi v Daniel Kapi and Electoral Commission* (SC 122 of 1998). Again the Supreme Court rejected the application. The court said:

> The discretion of the Court under the "slip" rule to correct errors is for the purpose of ensuring that the decision of the court reflects the judgment made by it. It is not to enable changes on law or

substance under that decision, such that the result would be a reversal or variation of it.

The new rules seek to codify the grounds for granting a review in the first instance. But it is silent on the issue of the "slip rule". It is suggested that the reason may be that because there will now be stringent rules regulating election reviews, the "slip rule" may become insignificant.

There are other issues such as legal costs, security for costs, local-level government elections, and election and leadership issues which are also covered by the authors in the text. For instance, the representation of lawyers, especially foreign legal counsels, in election petitions is opposed by Narakobi. He argues in Chapter 5 that because foreign lawyers have limited local knowledge they should not appear in election petitions.

Security for cost is an important issue for all the parties involved in election disputes. The Chief Justice and Kwa in Chapters 3 and 6 respectively discuss the adverse impacts high legal costs have on the disputing parties.

Election disputes are not only a national issue. They are also very vibrant at the local level. Gelu provides very alarming statistics in Chapter 1 about the volume of election petitions that were filed in the District Courts after the 1997 Elections. In comparison to the 89 petitions filed at the National Court there was a total of 435 petitions filed in the District Courts throughout the country. This is certainly an astronomical figure and clearly shows the interrelationship between national and local politics.

The problem of election violence and intimidation through the use of guns can be reduced if candidates are able to exercise control and good judgment in the elections. The Chief Ombudsman makes it clear in Chapter 8 that if candidates allow these things to happen and then get elected into Parliament they will face the full force of the law. The Chief Ombudsman calls on prospective leaders to be diligent, honest and self-controlled during the elections and also after the elections. Anno Pala picks up the call by the Chief Ombudsman in Chapter 9 and also explains that elected leaders must show responsibility even after they are elected to Parliament because their conduct will be closely monitored through the auspices of the *Organic Law on the Integrity of Political Parties and Candidates* (OLIPPC).

The message from Geno and Pala is very clear. Papua New Guinea needs honest and incorruptible leadership. And this can only be achieved if the people use good judgment in the elections, and the authorities responsible for implementing the law are diligent in performing their duties.

The final comment we want to make is in relation to the impact of the *Aigru* case. Shephard discusses the impact of this decision on the OLIPPC and concludes that the Organic Law may be unconstitutional. The wider implications of this case on other Organic Laws and particularly the OLNLGE is very disconcerting. A losing candidate may well argue that using the *Agiru* test, certain provisions of the OLNLGE on the election process are not authorized by sections 12, 125 and 126 of the *Constitution* and thus, unconstitutional and invalid. If this argument is successful the whole 2002 Elections will be thrown into chaos. There is therefore, an urgent need to rectify this decision either through the Parliament exercising its law-making powers to make an amendment to section 12 of the Constitution or through innovative judicial law-making.

Notes

1. Sections 57 and 58 of the Constitution vest the duty on the National Court and the Supreme Court to enforce the constitutional rights of Papua New Guineans.

2. See the discussion of constitutional rights in Kwa, EL, *Constitutional Law of Papua New Guinea* (Sydney: Law Book Company Ltd, 2001) 140. See also Kwa, EL, "Enforcement of Human Rights in Papua New Guinea: Tru O Giaman?" in Kwa, EL, Bhalla, S, Muroa, G, Tennent, D, Yapao, G (ed) *Development of Administrative Law in Papua New Guinea* (New Delhi: School of Law and Business Studies—UPNG and UBSPD, 2000) 179.
3. For instance see the cases, *Re Organic Law on National Elections* [1982] PNGLR 289 and *SCR No 5 of 1992* [1992] PNGLR 114.
4. The principles of this case are discussed by Kwa and Golman in Chapter 2.
5. The Committee comprised members of the judiciary and the PNG Law Society. The members were Justice T, Hinchliffee (Chairman); Justice B, Sakora; Justice M, Sevua; Justice S, Injia; Dr. J, Nonggorr; Mr. A, Manase, Ms. E, Dirua and Mr. C, Narakobi.

Contents

Part One

Elections in Papua New Guinea: An Overview

Chapter One

The Conduct of Elections in Papua New Guinea

*Gelu, A**

Introduction

Papua New Guinea (PNG) became an independent State on 16th September 1975. Unlike other former colonies, the process of decolonization in Papua New Guinea was peaceful and without bloodshed. The power and authority of government was formally transferred to the indigenous leaders who had familiarized themselves with the Western institutions and processes. As such, the establishment of the democratic order which began soon after the Second World War flourished.

An important element of the democratic order was the conduct of elections which for PNG began with the 1964 elections. This election brought to fore other components of democracy such as universal suffrage and the act of voting itself. The application of the universal suffrage, which provided the impetus for eligible voters to vote, was the beginning of the induction of the populace into the democratic political culture. At the same time, the act of voting, which was a new phenomenon in selecting leaders, was introduced as well as the use of the secret ballot.[1] Since 1964, two other elections were conducted before independence.[2] After 1975 five national elections were conducted.[3] The sixth national election will be held in 2002.

The conduct of elections is an important aspect of modern political systems. Whether a system is democratic or not, elections are conducted to legitimize the authority of those individuals and groups who are selected to represent the populace. Despite the similarity of the legitimization of the regimes in democratic systems as well as undemocratic systems, there are vast differences in the conduct of elections in the two regimes. The main difference is that elections in democratic regimes are usually competitive and free from manipulation from those in power as well as those who are intending to hold public offices. While in undemocratic regimes, elections are rigged and intended to serve the purpose of legitimizing the authority of the rulers or cliques. The principles of free and fair elections are the goals of a democratic election. Hence, there are important universal elements that would make an election free and fair. And any practice that does not conform to the accepted processes of electioneering would eventually affect that goal.

These practices can take various forms. These may include intimidation and violence which are not only common in undemocratic countries, but also in many democratic countries such as PNG. This suggestion creates a dilemma for countries like PNG and others which have a democratic system of government. This is because the process of selecting its leaders is highly dubious. This is evident in the numerous abuses and limited competition by political parties.

What is an election and what are its functions? What are the main elements of an election? How has PNG featured in the process of free and fair election? What does the increase in the large number of electoral disputes suggest with regard to the conduct of elections in PNG? These are the questions that will be discussed in this chapter.

Functions of an Election

Elections are conducted to satisfy certain democratic requirements. The democratic requirements therefore, imply that an election has important functions in a democracy. According to Harrop and Miller there are two contrasting views of the function of competitive elections. Firstly, elections are a mechanism through which politicians can be called to account and forced to introduce policies that reflect the wishes of the people. Secondly, the election is a means through which governments and political elite can exercise control over the people.[4] However, in reality, elections have no single character. Like all channels of political communication, elections are a two-way street that provides the government and the people, the elite and the masses, an opportunity to influence one another.

The main functions of elections according to Heywood include the following:[5]

- Recruiting politicians: In democratic states, elections are the principal source of political recruitment. This is seen through the process of parties nominating candidates, thus recruiting potential leaders. Intending candidates and eventually politicians possess talents and skills that make them appeal to the people. Elections do not fill posts that require specialized knowledge or experience, such as those in the civil service or judiciary.[6]
- Making governments: Elections directly make governments such as in the United States where the President is directly elected. In parliamentary democracies such as Britain, Australia, New Zealand, PNG and so on, elections influence the formation of governments. The activity of 'horse trading' in PNG is an example of this function.

- Providing representation: When elections are fair and competitive, they are a means through which demands are channeled from the public to the government. It is therefore necessary for the government to ensure that it governs according to the wishes of the people.
- Influencing policy: Elections can give the people the opportunity to influence decisions of the parties who would eventually become part of the government. Despite the fact that society at large has marginal influence over the policy priorities of parties, the votes would indicate whether it approves of a particular policy or not.
- Educating voters: The process of campaigning provides the electorate with an abundance of information about parties, candidates, policies, the current government's record, the political system and so on.
- Building legitimacy: One reason why even undemocratic regimes bother to hold elections, even though they are non-competitive, is that elections help to foster legitimacy by providing justification for a system of rule.
- Strengthening the elite: Elections can also be a vehicle through which elites can manipulate and control the people. This is one case against elections that are seen as a constitutional or legal means of controlling the people and making them believe that they have some control over who should govern.

The above functions of the election provide us with the opportunity to see why elections are important and necessary.

Elements of Democratic Elections

What are the essential elements of a free election? According to Ranney, the first major element is to hold regular elections. That is elections must take place regularly within prescribed time limits and may not be postponed indefinitely by public officials whenever they wish. Secondly, meaningful choices should be available, which means that voters must have a choice in casting their votes on a number of competing candidates.[7] These elements are important as they define the nature and scope of a free election.

Thirdly, there must be freedom for groups to put forth their candidates. No group(s) should be denied the right to nominate their candidates to contest a particular seat. Fourthly, there must be freedom to know and discuss the choices. This means that all the candidates must be given the opportunity to sell their ideas to the voters and the voters must not be denied the right to listen to different ideas. The fifth element is the use of the universal adult suffrage concept. This is a democratic idea, which states that all the eligible voting population have the right to vote.

The sixth element is the equal weighting of votes. One of the basic principles of democracy is political equality – the principle that each adult citizen must have the same opportunity as every other adult citizen to participate in the political decision-making process. When applied to elections, the principle means that all adults must not only have an equal opportunity to register their choices by voting, but also that each person's vote will have the same weight as every other person's vote. If some people's votes are weighted more heavily than the others, the principle of political equality is violated and the favoured voters constitute a kind of oligarchy[8] or ruling elite.

The seventh element of a democratic election is the free registration of choices. This means that voters must vote without fear for whichever candidates they wish to vote. There should not be any fear or coercion applied on the voters. The final element of a democratic election is the accurate counting of choices and the reporting of results. This means that counting procedures must provide accurate totals of the preferences registered for each alternative. And reporting procedures must guarantee that the totals, which control who wins the contested office, are honestly published. Butler listed the following requirements for a democratic election:[9]

- All adults have the right to vote.
- Regular elections occur within prescribed time limits.
- All the seats in the legislature are subject to election and are usually contested.
- No substantial group is denied the opportunity of forming a party and putting forward candidates.
- The electoral administration must be 'reasonably fair': neither law, nor violence, nor intimidation should bar candidates from presenting and discussing the views of voters.
- Voters should cast their votes freely and secretly, the votes counted and reported honestly, and converted into legislative seats as prescribed by law.
- Those elected should be installed in office and remain in office until their terms expire or a new election is held.

The requirements of a democratic election or competitive election provided by Butler have proven useful for determining the outlook or conduct of an election that is democratic. Thus, political scientists generally agree on what comprises a democratic election as indicated by the two authors. Robert Dahl has made a significant contribution to the discussion of a democratic election where he identifies and discusses seven characteristics[10] in his discussion of a 'polyarchy'[11]. These seven characteristics are: government is in the hands of elected officials; elections are free and fair; practically all adults have the right to vote; The right to run for office is unrestricted; there is free expression and a right to criticize and protest; citizens have access to alternative sources of information; and groups and associations enjoy at least relative independence from government.[12]

To sustain free and democratic elections, the wider political environment must also meet certain conditions. Political democracy like economic development needs some infrastructure. Mackenzie lists four such conditions:

- An independent judiciary to interpret electoral laws.
- An honest, competent and non-partisan administration to run elections.
- A developed system of political parties where political parties are well organized to put their policies and leaders before the electors as alternatives to choose from.
- An acceptance throughout the political community of certain rules of the game which regulate and limit the struggle for power.[13]

These conditions would assist the conduct of an election that will be truly free and fair. The absence of one of these conditions would undermine the democratic outcome of the election and the democratic process as a whole. For an independent judiciary, this is important when it comes to interpreting the laws when dealing with election disputes. In PNG where elections have created more disputes, the role and contribution of the judiciary is vital.

Having an honest, competent and non-partisan institutions to manage elections is also crucial. This will allow the institutions to carry out functions such as voter registration without any interference from political parties and candidates. In PNG, it is the Electoral Commission which performs this function and over the years it has tried its best to ensure that the elections are conducted in a democratic manner. This function is vested in the Electoral Commission by the *Organic Law on National and*

Local-level Government Elections (OLNLGE). Section 15 of the Organic Law states that, it is the primary function of the Electoral Commission to organize and conduct all elections for the Parliament and the legislative arms of the local-level governments.

A developed system of political parties is equally important to provide an environment that is conducive for the people to participate meaningfully in the political process. Political parties should provide the voters adequate information on what they are going to do once elected into office. This would come in the form of party policies or platforms. This also gives the voters the chance to select candidates of their own choices. In order to achieve this, the parties have to use various means of communication to disseminate information to the people. The various forms of the media, especially the radio, have been commonly used. In PNG this factor has been limited in the previous elections. The party system is not well developed in the sense that the parties have not forged a link between themselves and the various interests groups in the society. It has been shown in previous studies[14] that they remain as parliamentary factions and are ideologically and organizationally weak. The effects of the *Organic Law on the Integrity of Political Parties and Candidates* (OLIPPC)[15] are yet to be realized. At the same time, the political parties have not embarked on an aggressive campaign to adequately inform the people of their policies as well as what they would do when they are voted into office. This has affected the ability of the voters to cast their votes according to their party preferences.

The acceptance of rules by the political community to limit the struggle for power is important. This idea points to the concept of the 'rule of law', a principle which requires that every one is equal before the law. In PNG, this concept has been adopted under section 37 of the *Constitution*. However, in practice the concept is usually abrogated and is abused throughout the country. It is widely accepted that the authority of the state and its laws has not been respected. This is evident in the rising law and order problems in the country. Practices such as voter intimidation, double voting and election violence frequently occur during the elections. Unfortunately no serious attempts have been made to address them.

Free and Fair Elections in Papua New Guinea

Are elections in PNG free and fair and are they competitive? In theory, the answer to the question is affirmative, especially when one examines the law governing the conduct of elections in PNG. The relevant law is the OLNLGE. The Organic Law clearly spells out how elections are to be conducted in the country. It also empowers the Electoral Commission to administer the conduct of elections in PNG. This legal authority enables the Electoral Commission to ensure that the elections are conducted fairly and freely. The OLNLGE has 21 parts which deal specifically with the various aspects of the electoral process. The organization of the common roll, the protection of polling officials and ballot boxes, the role of scrutineers, the organization of polling booths, disputing election results and other related matters are covered by the OLNLGE.

Elections in PNG are competitive in the sense that they provide the voters alternate information (but sometimes very limited) and a large pool of candidates to choose from. Despite the failure of the party system to provide a range of choice in terms of their policies to the voters, the parties still influence to some extent, as to how the people cast their votes. However, when it comes to the question of whether the elections held since 1975 were free and fair, it is suggested that they were not. Several election reports by the Electoral Commission as well as reports by various commentators[16] show that elections in PNG have not been democratic. The reports have shown that in one way or another, the elections have been marred with practices that undermined the principles of free and fair elections. The proliferation of these practices is institutionalized and is deemed unconventional to the democratic process. These practices which include electoral violence, intimidation of voters and electoral officials, corruption and lack of accountability, failure to represent the interest of the people, disregard for established procedures and laws, and so forth have been prominent. The occurrences of these practices have affected the manner in which elections are conducted and these consequences have given rise to unorthodox practices that are uncommon to developed democracies. In the 1997 Election Report to Parliament the Electoral Commission noted that:

> ...a long standing problem that interferes with the conduct of free and fair elections in Papua New Guinea and hence, detracts from the legitimating effect of those elections, is the incidence of election-related violence, whether before, during or after polling[17]...

The national media has documented fully the extent of election-related violence; intimidation of voters and electoral officials, particularly through the use of weapons; murders; unauthorized roadblocks; snatching of ballot papers and ballot boxes.

The Electoral Commission reported that it has faced many difficult problems relating to elections over the years. The most common problems faced by the polling officials are:

- stealing of ballot papers and ballot boxes;
- rioting between tribal or ethnic groups during polling;
- harassment and intimidation of polling officials with guns, knives and axes;

- exerting force on polling officials to use all available ballot papers issued to the team at one polling place; and
- allowing one person to mark every ballot paper on behalf of every illiterate voter.[18]

The Electoral Commission lost many ballot boxes and ballot papers during the process of polling through attacks made on the teams. Criminal gangs and supporters of candidates initiated most of these attacks. In addition, tribal fights or ethnic clashes have often disrupted smooth polling and in most cases polling teams refused to return to the area in fear of their lives. According to the Electoral Commission:

> ...intimidation and harassment of polling officials are the order of the day in almost every election we have conducted so far in Papua New Guinea. The exerting of unnecessary force on polling officials under gun point to use all ballot papers have denied those voters in the next allocated polling area. To make matters worse, in some polling areas, one single person is earmarked to mark every ballot paper for every voter who could not read or write as well as handicapped voters. Despite the presence of the police, electoral rules are often ignored.[19]

The final observation made by the Electoral Commission was supported by the Commonwealth Observatory Group when it wrote that in rural areas where the numbers of illiterate voters were highest:

> ...we noticed that the same person sometimes made repeated visits to the polling booth accompanied by a different voter each time. This gave rise to the suspicion that these helpers could have been working for a particular candidate and that they were ensuring that

voters cast their ballot for that candidate. In some place more than one 'helper' attempted to accompany the voter.[20]

The Commonwealth Group further observed that while the ballot was genuinely secret, in some parts of the Highlands, for instance, it was not. Voting compartments or screens were not used, so voting was not done in private the ballot paper was marked at a table within sight of anyone who cared to watch.

The Commonwealth Group also noted that election violence in PNG have been predominant in some parts of the country. At the same time, the Group observed that there were allegations of campaign abuses including bribery and threats, the calling-in of favours, campaigning past polling day and nomination of friendly candidates to split votes. While the splitting of votes is not illegal, it has greatly affected the margins of winners and raised doubts on the mandate that the winners have.

One major area that the Electoral Commission needs to improve on is the proper updating of the Common Roll. This process is important to sustaining democracy[21] because it affects the ability of the people to vote and at the same time it excludes people from voting as a means to participating in the political process. The improper update of the Common Roll has resulted in many people being turned away at the polling places. This anomaly was more predominant in the 1997 Elections than in previous elections.[22] This was due, partly to the failure of successive governments to conduct a census before an election. The Commonwealth Group discovered that in some cases, presiding officers who had disallowed a large number of apparently qualified persons from voting (because they were not on the Common Roll) resorted to the use of the 1992 Common Roll. The Group also discovered that there was both under registration in particular areas and over registration in others. As a result, ghost names, double registration and dramatic increase in the size of the Common Roll were discovered in some areas.

These problems have caused difficulties for the Electoral Commission and also for every one participating in the electoral process. For a developing democracy, something drastic has to be done to ensure that elections are free and fair. This depends very much on the ability of the national government acting through the Electoral Commission to formulate appropriate strategies to curtail these problems.

While the change to the voting system has been given prominence, this would have a limited effect on the processes of free and fair election. The experience throughout the world is that regardless of the type of voting system, the democraticness of an election can only be determined by the manner in which it has been conducted.

Election Disputes

What have been the consequences of failing to adhere to the practices of free and fair elections as outlined by the OLNLGE? The result is the increasing number of disputes challenging the validity of Elections results. The process of election dispute is recognised and allowed by the law to ensure that the election process is free and fair. In PNG, election disputes have become a norm after each Elections and the incidences of such cases have increased over time. As noted by Ray Anere, there were 42 election disputes recorded after the 1987 Elections, 67 after the 1992 Elections and 89 after the 1997 Elections.[23]

The Electoral Commission has indicated that a total of 89 election petitions were filed in the national court after the 1997 national election challenging the results of a number of seats.[24] In the ensuing trials, increasing the total election cases number to 114.

The situation is even more serious considering the number of petitions lodged after the conduct of local-level government elections soon after the 1997 National Elections.[25] The Electoral Commission noted that a staggering 435 petitions were lodged in the District Courts, creating a nightmare for the Electoral Commission and the country generally. A total of 284 urban and rural local-level governments comprising 5747 wards were contested. Although the wards are geographically small compared to the Open Electorates, heavy campaigning and lobbying which are usually the trademarks of national elections were also observed in the local-level government elections. It is no wonder that many of the results for the local-level governments were disputed.

The distribution of the 435 petitions filed were as follows:

- Southern Highlands – 77
- Enga – 75
- East Sepik – 43
- Eastern Highlands – 36
- Morobe – 34
- Oro – 25
- Western Highlands – 22
- East New Britain – 17
- Simbu – 17
- Sandaun – 17
- Madang – 14
- Gulf – 12
- New Ireland – 9
- West New Britain – 9
- Central – 8
- Western – 8
- Manus – 7

- National Capital District Commission – 2
- Motu-Koitabu – 2

From the total number of petitions, 60 were struck out, eight were withdrawn, another eight were dismissed and two were upheld. By October 1999 a total of 356 petitions remained unresolved.

The conclusion that can be drawn from the above figures is that, apart from the Milne Bay Province, every other province experienced an immediate increase in election petitions for local government seats with the passage of the OLNLGE. This large number of petitions for local-level government seats highlights the intricate linkages that exist between national politics and local practices. This is part of a growing trend or culture which is that whatever happens at the centre will also have a spiral effect on the periphery. That is, practices that are widely used at the national level are now also being used at the local level. For instance, election disputes which are common in elections to the Parliament are rapidly emerging at the local level. Two examples of other practices that have impacted local-level governments are the vote of no-confidences against presidents of local-level governments and political interferences in the administration of local governments.

In a recent development, the Supreme Court ruled that the 1997 Rural Local-level Government Elections in Aitape East, Aitape West, West Wapei and East Wapei covering a total of 80 wards in the Sandaun Province was null and void. As a result of the decision, by-elections will be held to fill all 80 vacant seats.[26] This exercise will be time consuming and costly to the Provincial Government and the Electoral Commission.

Beside the huge costs involved in conducting by-elections, the issue of representation also features prominently. Election petitions have led to some electorates not being represented. As it currently stands, Madang has not been able to have a Provincial Member after Jim Kas (the Provincial Member) was ousted from office. The people of Imbongu in the Southern Highlands province were left in a confused state after the sitting Member Peter Peipul was ousted from office by Pila Nininga (a petitioner). However, Niningi lasted as a Member of Parliament for only a few weeks because on appeal the Supreme Court reinstated Peipul as the duly elected member for Imbongu Open. This particular electorate is now without a representative in Parliament because Peter Peipul was recently dismissed as a Member of Parliament by the Leadership Tribunal. The people of Southern Highlands have also lost their Provincial Member, Mr. Anderson Agiru because he was also dismissed by the Leadership Tribunal.

Thus, election petitions have proven to be a very time consuming and expensive exercise. Moreover, election disputes cause a lot of uncertainty in the minds of the voters and also impose unnecessary burden on the elected Member of Parliament or the local-level government.

Conclusion

The conduct of elections in PNG have been outlined in this chapter. The major requirements of a democratic election as well as the functions of elections have been discussed to assist in understanding the conduct of elections in Papua New Guinea since 1977.

From the foregoing discussions it is suggested that the election process in the country is becoming more undemocratic as the years have gone bye. This has significantly affected the conduct of elections that are supposed to be free and fair. The high incidences of election disputes clearly indicate that elections are not free and fair.

The reports by the Electoral Commission and various commentators suggest that the elections are not free and fair in PNG. As a result, election disputes have increased to an extent that it is taking up most of the time of the courts as well as the resources of the Electoral Commission and the disputants. It is even more serious at the local-level governments. Based on the alarming figures provided by the Electoral Commission on the number of election disputes arising after the 1997 Elections, it is suggested that the elections conducted for local-level governments were far less democratic.

There is little doubt that despite the clarity of the law governing the conduct of elections, the people (voters), the candidates and the political parties continue to abuse the law. The law has a simple function, and that is, to ensure that elections are free and fair. Once these rules are ignored, the end result will be the increasing number of election disputes. Hopefully the government will seriously look at this problem and address it accordingly. Failure to do this would affect not only the democratic make-up of our society, but also more specifically the conduct of elections which are supposed to be free and fair.

Notes

* Ph.D candidate, Department of Political Science, The University of Auckland, New Zealand. I would like to thank Mr. Eric Kwa, former Executive Dean of the School of Law and Business and now a PhD candidate at the Faculty of Law, University of Auckland for inviting me to make this contribution to the book.

1. The people did vote, but the fairness of the act itself has been questioned, especially with regard to the use of whispering ballot as opposed to the secret ballot.
2. 1968 and 1972.
3. 1977, 1982, 1987, 1992 and 1997.
4. Harrop, M and Millar, W, *Election and Votes: A Comparative Introduction* (Houndsmill: Macmillan, Houndsmill, 1987), 9.

5. Heywood, A, *Politics* (Houndsmill: Macmillan Press, 1987), 213.
6. This area of electioneering is problematic in PNG where former politicians have been appointed to head statutory bodies as well as diplomatic posts.
7. Ranney, A, *Governing: An Introduction to Political Science* (Berkeley: University of California, 1990), 173.
8. It means: government by the few who govern in their own interest.
9. Butler, D, "Electoral Systems" in Harrop, M and Miller, W, above n. 4 at p. 7. These elements of a democratic elections were also discussed by Gelu in Gelu, A, "The Emergence of a Non-Liberal Democratic Political Culture in Papua New Guinea" in Rynkiewich, W and Seib, R (ed), *Politics in Papua New Guinea: Continuities, Changes and Challenges* (Point No. 24) (Goroka: Melanesian Institute, 2000) 94.
10. Dahl, R, *Democracy and its Critics* (New Haven: Yale University Press, 1989).
11. It literally means 'rule by the many' and it refers to institutions and political processes of modern representative democracy.
12. Full discussion of these characteristics can also be found in Gelu, above, n. 9 at pp. 96-97.
13. Mackenzie, W, "Free Elections" in Harrop, M and Millar, above, n. 4 at p. 7.
14. See Turner, M and Hegarty, D, *The 1987 National Elections in Papua New Guinea* (Canberra: The Australian Institute of International Affairs, 1987).
15. This Organic Law was passed only in 2001 and will be in effect during and after the 2002 Election.
16. See Hegarty, D, *Electoral Politics in Papua New Guinea: Studies on the 1977 National Elections*, (Port Moresby: UPNG Press, 1983); King, D, *Pangu Returns to Power: The 1982 Elections in Papua New Guinea* (Canberra: ANU, 1989); Oliver, M, *Eleksin: The 1987 National Election in Papua New Guinea* (Port Moresby: UPNG Press, 1989) and Saffu, Y, *The 1992 PNG Election: Change and Continuity in Electoral Politics* (Canberra: ANU, 1996).

17. The PNG Electoral Commission, *Report to the Sixth Parliament on the 1997 National Election* (Port Moresby: Electoral Commission, July 1997), p. 5.
18. Electoral Commission of Papua New Guinea, "Preparing for the 2002 National and Local Level Government Elections" (National Legal Convention, 5th - 6th, November, 2001), p. 7.
19. Ibid.
20. The Commonwealth Secretariat, *The Report of the Commonwealth Observer Group, The General Election in Papua New Guinea: 14-28 June 1997* (London, Commonwealth Secretariat, 1997), p. 26-27.
21. An important element of modern democracy is that it is inclusive rather than exclusive. This process came about in the late 1900s when universal suffrage was accorded to every eligible adult as compared to the previous practice of voting based on certain entitlements.
22. I was one of those thousands of eligible voters who did not vote because my name was not on the Common Roll.
23. Anere, A, "Political Parties and Elections in Papua New Guinea" in Rynkiewich, W and Seib, R, above, n. 9 at p. 133.
24. *The Voter* (Issue No. 7), October 1999, p. 7.
25. Ibid.
26. Ibid.

Chapter Two

Legal Framework for Resolving Election Disputes in Papua New Guinea

*Kwa, EL and Golman, W**

This chapter provides an overview of the election review process beginning with the initiation of an election petition in the National Court to its completion in the Supreme Court. A brief discussion about the shift in the law from the *Organic Law on National Elections* (OLNE) to the *Organic Law on National and Local-level Government Elections* (OLNLGE) is also provided in this chapter. Also a short discussion on the election disputes at the Local-level Government as provided for under the OLNLGE is set out in this chapter.

Preliminary Issues

The election process in PNG is an important component of the democratic process in the country. Formal voting first emerged in the country in the 1964 Elections for the Legislative Council. This democratic process was also applied in the 1968 and 1972 Elections.

After the 1972 Elections, the House of Assembly established the Constitutional Planning Committee (CPC) and tasked it with the responsibility of formulating a constitution for a new state to be called Papua New Guinea.[1] The CPC then toured the country gauging the views of the people with the view to formulating the *constitution* for the country.

The CPC found that the overwhelming majority of the people wanted the new emerging country to adopt and apply democratic principles. One of the pillars of democracy that the people wanted in the new state was the conduct of democratic elections to choose leaders of the country. The views of the people are reflected in various sections of the *Constitution*. These provisions are sections 50, 103, 105, 125 and 126. Section 50 guarantees the citizens the right to vote and stand for public office. This provision outlaws the occupation of public offices including seats in Parliament through arbitrary and illegal means. Sections 103 and 105 set out the qualifications required to stand for elections. The final provisions provide the framework for the conduct of national elections.

The relevant law that deals primarily with national elections is the *Organic Law on National and Local Level Government Elections* 1997 (OLNLGE). This Organic Law gives effect to sections 125[2] and 126 of the *Constitution*.

The conduct of elections in PNG is the responsibility of the Electoral Commission created by section 5 of the OLNLGE. Section 15 of the Organic Law vests the Commission with the primary function of organizing and conducting all elections for the national Parliament and local-level governments. Before a national election, the Electoral Commission is required to make available appropriate number of personnel to effectively and properly conduct the election.[3]

The conduct of national elections in PNG can sometimes be difficult because of the geography of the country, the high illiteracy rate, election violence,[4] updating of the Common Roll[5] and limited funds and resources. Some of these problems are often created by the Electoral Commission itself. For instance, Ketan and Mangi observed that simple logistical problems such as shortage of ballot papers and ink used to identify voters could have been overcome if the Electoral Commission had taken extra care to provide extra supplies.[6] Some of these problems can prove fatal to an election such as in the cases of *Thomas Sumuno v Louis Ambane & the Electoral Commission* (1998) N1718 and *David Basua and Ors v Charles Miru* (SCR 62, 79 and 92 of 1998). In the first case there were insufficient ballot boxes so the presiding officers stored the excess ballot papers in some patrol boxes without the authorization of the Electoral Commissioner. The ballot papers in the unofficial patrol boxes were pivotal in determining the outcome of the petition. In this case the ballot papers in the unofficial boxes were counted and the result was that the petitioner won by more than 200 votes. The election of Louis Ambane was therefore, declared void and a by-election ordered. On review in *Louis Ambane and Electoral Commission v Thomas Sumono* (1998) SC 559, the Supreme Court rejected the application by the applicants to reverse the order of the National Court.

It is important to note that where the peoples' right to vote entrenched under section 50 is violated by the actions or omissions of the Electoral Commission, this breach can be used as a ground to vitiate an election. In other cases however, where the act or omission does not impact on the outcome of the elections, the elections will not be voided.

The Electoral Commission has been the subject of criticisms over the years. The main criticism has been directed at its efficiency and professionalism in conducting general elections. In a scathing attack on the Electoral Commission, the Chief Justice said:

> I would like to make some observation about the conduct of this Electorate's election which is common to a number of other electorates' election being reviewed by the courts. ...The Electoral Commission has had five years to prepare for this election. It is

> unacceptable that costly elections have to be voided because of this kind of administrative inefficiency, that results in a large number of votes being excluded, affecting the result as they have in this case and necessitating another expensive election.[7]

The Chief Justice was also critical of the Electoral Commission when he made the same observation in another election blunder by the Commission in *David Basua and Ors v Charles Miru* (supra). The Prime Minister, Sir Morauta, was also critical of the Commission and the electoral system, arguing strongly that the current electoral system was a *fuss* and should be abandoned soon.[8] He recommended *an on-line decentralized, continuous and national enrolment system* to be used for the 2002 General Election and beyond.

The Prime Minister's sentiments were quickly supported by various sectors of the community including Lady Carol Kidu, the Member for Port Moresby South in the Parliament.[9] Similar concerns were also raised by the Commonwealth Observer Group in 1997. The Group's report revealed that the current Common Roll was flawed and required major reforms, especially in relation to registration and construction of the Common Roll.[10]

There is general agreement that the electoral system requires an overhaul. The Electoral Commission has to seriously identify its own deficiencies and rectify them before the next election this year. In the long term, it has to urgently review and identify the relevant weaknesses in the electoral system and propose drastic measures for approval before the 2007 National Election.

Redefining the Electoral Laws

In 1997, the OLNE which was enacted before independence in 1975 was repealed and replaced by the OLNLGE. The principal reason for the change in the law was to make provision for the election of local-level government members whose offices are created by the *Organic Law on Provincial and Local-level Governments* (OLPLLG). This new addition to the law is located in Part XIX of the OLNLGE.

Apart from the insertion of Part XIX, does the OLNLGE differ in any detail from the OLNE? As will be shown throughout this chapter the answer is obviously negative. The next question is: has the law on election petition changed? Unfortunately, there is no substantial shift in the law relating to election petitions. The procedure for conducting an election petition and the factors that give rise to an election petition, and the law that clarifies the process have remain unchanged.

There are, however, three minor changes which have been made to the election petition process. The first shift relates to section 208(d). In the former Organic Law the time period for lodging an election petition was four months. In a standard calendar year, a month would have 30 or 31 days hence, four months would give 122 days altogether. Under the OLNLGE the time period has been reduced to only 40 days.[11] This is a reduction of 82 days. This change was aimed at limiting the propensity of losing candidates using the four months to cause unnecessary delays in filing an election petition and also to expedite the election dispute process. The 40 days time limit according to the Supreme Court in *Application by Julius Chan* (SCR 71 of 1997) can be extended if the thirty-ninth and fortieth days fall on a weekend. It is imperative to observe that the Supreme Court did not say that the 40 days do not include weekends. The 40 days include weekends, but if the last or second last day falls on a weekend, the following Monday and the Tuesday (whichever the case) can be counted as the fortieth day or the thirty-ninth and fortieth days.

The second change is found in section 209. Although the new section 209 is the exact replica of the former section

209 of the OLNE, the amount of security deposit has been increased from K2000 to K2500. The increase in this fee is aimed at discouraging losing candidates from initiating frivolous and unmeritorious petitions. Unfortunately, this increase in fees has not deterred the number of losing candidates challenging the election results as highlighted by the 89 petitions filed in the National Court after the 1997 Election.

The third change relates to the referral in section 208(d) in both the repealed OLNE and the current OLNLGE. That is, under the former, the reader is directed to section 176(1)(a) while under the latter, the reader is referred to section 175(1)(a). However, the wordings are the same in both provisions. Apart from these, there are no alteration in the structure, meanings and arrangements of the provisions.

The parts and divisions dealing with election petitions under these two Organic Laws are exactly the same. It is therefore, clear that the statute law on election petitions has not shifted drastically since 1975.

The Legal Framework on Election Disputes

Disputing an election is a serious business because it is a very expensive, time consuming and sometimes a painful proceeding. As the Supreme Court expressed in *Re Delba Biri v Bill Ninkama*:

> It seems to us that the statute has clearly expressed its intention that a petition must strictly comply with s 208. It is not difficult to see why an election petition is not an ordinary cause and it is a very serious thing.[12]

Under the new Organic Law the same principles have been adopted by the Supreme Court in *Application of Albert Karo* (SCR 48 of 1998). In this instance, the Supreme Court stated that, "[An] election is a very serious matter because in effect the petition challenges the express views of the majority of the people. An election petition is not an ordinary case".

This view entrenched the position that because election petitions are serious cases, stringent conditions should be imposed on the process of determining the outcome of the petition. This view is in direct contradiction to the original aim of the election petition process as designated under the OLNE which has been retained in large part by the OLNLGE. The original intent of the Organic Law was to remove lawyers from the election review process. Thus, where a petitioner comes to the court without legal representation and the court finds that the petition was drafted clumsily the court must proceed to entertain the petition. This exposition of the law was made by the Supreme Court in *Electoral Commission and Henry Smith v Bire Kimisopa* (SCR 93 of 1997).

Given the seriousness of election petitions, a petitioner has to be mindful of the procedure for filing a petition and the matters that comprise the document called the election petition. There are several important issues that need to be highlighted before we proceed to deal with the elements of an election petition. These are: (1) the correct forum; (2) legal representation; (3) legal costs, and (4) finality of the decision of the National Court.

The Court of Disputed Returns

An election petition is initiated by addressing the petition to the National Court. The "National Court sitting as a Court of Disputed Returns is a creature of statute [OLNLGE]".[13] This is the clear intent of section 206 of the OLNLGE. The role of the court is to ensure that the election was conducted fairly and properly. In performing its functions, section 217 directs that the National Court is not strictly bound by legal forms or technicalities or whether the evidence before it is in accordance with the law of evidence or not. The court must be fair, flexible and be guided by substantial merits and good conscience when it is dealing with a petition. This is an onerous responsibility. The Supreme Court expressed this point more firmly in *Application of Albert Karo* (SCR 48 of 1998) where it said, "under the Organic Law [OLNLGE] the hearing of the election petition or dispute is the sole responsibility of the Judge of the National Court. The Judge is the master of that law and those actions completely". In dealing with election petitions, the National Court is not bound by the *National Court Rules*. This point of law was clarified by the Supreme Court in *Biri v Ninkama* [1982] PNLGR 342 and *Application by Electoral Commission* [1991] PNGLR 372, and lately in *Korak Yasona v Castan Maibawa and Electoral Commission* (SCR 81 of 1998).

The powers of the National Court are enumerated under sections 212 and 215. When seeking orders in an election petition, the petitioner must claim one or more of the remedies listed under these provisions. Prior to 1998, the rule was that a petition that does not seek any of the remedies listed by section 215 is defective and can be struck out. This law was pronounced by the Supreme Court in *Application of William Ekip Wii* (SCR 45 of 1994). However, this interpretation has now been rejected by the Supreme Court in *Korak Yasona v Castan Maibawa and Electoral Commission* (1998) SC 552. In the former case, the Supreme Court held that a petitioner must clearly state the remedies he or she seeks under section 215(1). If the petitioner does not specify the correct remedy under this provision, he or she will lose the case on this technicality, even though he or she succeeds on the substantive matter. In the latter case, the Supreme Court reversed its previous ruling because it said:

> It surely must be travesty of justice and not within the spirit of section 217 of the Organic Law [OLNLGE] to

administer "real justice", if bribery or undue influence were established to the entire satisfaction of the court pursuant to section 215(1) and yet the declaration that the election of the successful candidate is void, could not be upheld simply because the terms of the relief sought were not in the precise terms of section 215(1). The court is empowered to grant the relief by virtue of the provisions of section 215(1) under which the allegations are brought.

This shift in the law is the correct interpretation of section 215(1). The court also made it clear that, if the petitioner seeks a relief under section 212(1)(f) and (h) and not section 215(1), the court does have the jurisdiction to grant a relief under section 215(1) if the allegations are proven at the trial.

The powers of the National Court listed in sections 212 and 215 can, however, only apply after the election results are declared. Does this mean that the National Court cannot exercise its jurisdiction before the polling day, but after nomination have been declared under section 93 of the OLNLGE? In *Kevin Massive v Iambakey Okuk and Johanes Kenderop* [1985] PNGLR 263,[14] it was held that the National Court has jurisdiction to determine a person's qualifications to stand as a candidate in an election to Parliament after nominations have been declared under section 92 (now section 93) of the OLNE and before the commencement of polling.

It would appear that the court can intervene in the electoral process before and after an election. However, in *Philip Kapal v Jack Karali and the Electoral Commission* (1997) N1646 and *Ronald Rimbao v Maku Kopeyala and Ors* (1997) N1585, the National Court ruled that it could not interfere in the administrative functions of the Electoral Commission because the court was not permitted by the OLNLGE to stop the counting and correct an error by electoral officials respectively. Both the judges in these two cases held that an aggrieved candidate could avail himself or herself to the Court of Disputed Returns after the declaration of the election results.

It is important to make a distinction between the roles of the National Court prior to an election and during, and after an election. In the first situation, the National Court exercises all its powers as vested on it by the Constitution and the relevant statutes. In the two latter cases, the National Court functions as the Court of Disputed Returns and therefore, its powers and functions are limited to those stipulated by the OLNLGE. Thus, in *Philip Kapal v Jack Karali and the Electoral Commission and Ronald Rimbao v Maku Kopeyala and Ors*, the court could not intervene because by then the elections had proceeded and in its capacity as the Court of Disputed Returns, it was estopped from interfering in the election process because of the limitations set by the OLNLGE. In *Philip Kapal's* case, the court actually noted that the plaintiff could invoke the power of the National Court (*per se*) to correct an error of the Electoral Commission, but only through the judicial review process provided under the *National Court Rules* and not under the OLNLGE. This ruling finds its basis in section 135 of the *Constitution*. This provision stipulates that the "National Court has power to determine any question ...". This includes the power to determine the question of whether a candidate is qualified to be or to remain a Member of Parliament.

In contrast, the National Court has no power to order particulars in respect of an election petition filed pursuant to section 208 of the OLNLGE.[15] The court also has no power to allow an amendment of a petition after the period of 40 days after the declaration of the result of the election has been made. For example, in *Re Delba Biri v Bill Ninkama* (supra) the petitioner applied against the National Court's decision to allow a petition made or registered after the four months period (now 40 days) required under section 208(d) of the OLNE had lapsed. The Supreme Court held that the National Court had no power to entertain any amendment after the time limit set by statute had lapsed and therefore, dismissed the petition.

The Supreme Court has also clarified in the case of *Masket Iangalio v Electoral Commission and Ors* (1998) SC 568 that, the National Court has no jurisdiction to try two or more petitions for the same electorate where the grounds of the petitions are substantially different and separate lawyers and different reliefs are sought by the petitioners. This principle was adopted and applied in *David Basua and Ors v Charles Miru* (SCR 62, 79 and 92 of 1998).

Legal Representation

Section 222 of the OLNLGE stipulates that a party to a petition shall not, except by the consent of all parties or by the leave of the National Court, be represented by a counsel or solicitor. The intent and operation of this provision was discussed in *David Lambu v Peter Ipatas, Edward Komu & Electoral Commission* (1997) N1614. In this case the applicant who was a professional lawyer had stood for the Enga Regional Seat and lost the election to the first respondent. He appeared in person while the respondent, an ordinary citizen appeared also in person. The applicant argued that the respondent was an educated and an experienced businessman and thus, he was able to defend himself. The court said that, if it was to accede to the applicant's request, then the respondents would be unfairly disadvantaged because they would be up against an experienced legal practitioner. The court therefore, refused the application and granted leave to the respondents' lawyers to appear on their behalf.

Legal Costs

Election disputes has become a very attractive business for lawyers. On the other hand, they are also a very big burden on the disputants. As one disputing party remarked when asked about his case "all my funds have been exhausted paying very expensive legal fees".[16]

Legal costs, in particular security for costs, have even been used by some parties in several election petitions to stop aggrieved parties from exercising their constitutional right in seeking a review in the Supreme Court. This strategy was employed in *David Lambu v Peter Ipatas and Ors* (1999) SC 601 and *Parry Zeipi v Gabia Gagarimabu* (1999) SC 611. The rules for imposing and enforcing security for costs were laid down in *David Lambu v Peter Ipatas and Ors*. The issue before the court was whether the court should order and enforce the order for security for costs against the petitioner and thus, deny the applicant's right to seek a review by the Supreme Court. After considering the arguments, the court ruled that the ultimate test should be "whether it is in the interest of justice to make an order for security for costs having regard to all the circumstances of the case". Applying this test, the court rejected the application to order the applicant to pay the security for cost before he would be allowed to pursue his case before the Supreme Court. The same result was reached in *Parry Zeipi v Gabia Gagarimabu and Peter Launa v Yauwe Riyong and Electoral Commission* (SCR 133 of 1998).[17] The same line of argument was raised in *Peter Peipul v Pila Niningi and Electoral Commission* (1998) SC 580, but it was rejected by the Supreme Court.

The issue of security for costs has been dealt with sparingly by the courts. The courts will be swayed towards the defaulter if he or she can show that he or she has a meritorious case, and thus the non-payment of the costs should not be a bar to his or her application for review. However, where there are other compelling reasons to dismiss the case, the courts will also take into consideration the non-payment of legal costs as a ground to dismiss the review.

Finality of the Decision of the National Court

According to section 220, the decision of the National Court is final and is not subject to any appeal. This issue was addressed in the case of *Balakau v Paker & Openakali* [1983] PNGLR 242. In that case, the petitioner filed a petition in the National Court challenging the validity of the election results for the Enga Regional Seat. The National Court ordered a re-count which also confirmed that the respondent was the winner. The petitioner then appealed the decision by way of a notice of appeal filed at the Supreme Court. The Supreme Court held that the National Court's decision was final and cannot be questioned in any way. Consequently the appeal was dismissed.

The final decision of the National Court in an election petition must be communicated to the Parliament through the Clerk of Parliament. Section 232 sets out the requirement in the following terms:

> After the hearing and determination of a reference under this Division, the Registrar of the National Court shall promptly forward to the Clerk of Parliament and the Electoral Commissioner a copy of the order or declaration of the National Court.

The underpinning of this proviso is that it is the membership of the Parliament which is being disputed and therefore, the Parliament through the Clerk of Parliament must be aware of who the rightful Member of Parliament is for the electorate in dispute. The Organic Law is, however, silent on what the consequences will be if the Registrar of the National Court fails to inform the Parliament about the decision of the National Court.

Once the Court of Disputed Returns makes it ruling, it cannot be interfered in any way except by the Supreme Court in its review jurisdiction under section 155(2)(b) of the Constitution. In the case of *Jimson Sauk v Don Polye and Electoral Commission* (1999) SC 616, Sauk attempted to stay the order of the National Court invalidating his election as a Member of Parliament by seeking a review under section 155(2)(b) and asking the Supreme Court to invoke its power under section 155(4) of the *Constitution* to stay the order. At the time the National Court made its ruling, Sauk was a serving Minister in the government. The Supreme Court rejected his application because in its view "it would not be proper to utilise section 155(4) of the *Constitution* to defeat the clear dictates of section 220 of the OLNLGE". Louis Ambane, who was the Governor of Simbu, also tried to stay the order of the National Court declaring his election void in *Louis Ambane and Electoral Commission v Thomas Sumuno* (1998) SC 559. The Supreme Court also refused the application to stay the order of the National Court.

Although aggrieved parties have an opening under section 155(2)(b) to bypass the bar in section 220, the Supreme Court has shown that it will not extend this power to stifle with the express intent of section 220.

Initiating an Election Petition under the OLNLGE

Election petitions are creatures of statute. Under the OLNE, the process was set out in Part XVIII which contained sections 206 to 233. The same part and provisions have been adopted verbatim by the OLNLGE. Thus, election petitions under the new Organic Law begin with section 206 and run through to section 233. No new provisions have been added to Part XVIII nor have there been any repeal of the provisions. It is interesting to note that there is no change in the sequential arrangement of the provisions. That is, there is no obvious change from the OLNE to the OLNLGE. Apart from the minor adjustment to section 208, the wordings and arrangement of the sections are exactly the same as the OLNE.

The courts have held that the institution of an election petition under the OLNLGE is a right which must not be unnecessarily encumbered by various rules and practices such that a citizen is prevented from freely exercising this right.[18] An election petition is usually initiated after the declaration of an election result in a national election. The definition of an election petition is clarified under section 227 as "a petition disputing an Election or Return". A petition disputing a national election is addressed to the National Court pursuant to section 206 and for a petition disputing a local government election, it is addressed to the District Court as stipulated under section 287(3) of the OLNLGE.

The starting point is section 208 of the OLNLGE. The petitioner must strictly comply with the requirements of section 208. The provision is in the following terms:

A petition shall:

(a) set out the facts relied on to invalidate the election or return;
(b) specify the relief to which the petitioner claims to be entitled;
(c) be signed by a candidate at the election in dispute or a person who was qualified to vote at the election;
(d) be attested by two witnesses whose addresses and occupation are stated; and
(e) be filed at the registry of the National Court at Port Moresby or at the court house in any provincial headquarters within 40 days after the declaration of the result of the election in accordance with section 175(1)(a).

A petition must be filed with a security deposit of K2,500.00 as required by section 209 of the Organic Law. Section 210 declares that the requirements of sections 208 and 209 are mandatory. The two recent cases of *Greg Mongi v Benard Vogae and The Electoral Commission*[19] and *Karo v Kidu* [1997] PNGLR 28 have reaffirmed that this position has not changed because sections 208 and 209 are the exact replica of the repealed OLNE.

There are several common grounds which are usually raised by petitioners to dispute the election results. In this segment of the chapter we discuss only seven grounds. These grounds are: (1) undue influence; (2) bribery; (3) illegal conduct by voters; (4) treating; (5) procedural irregularities by electoral officials; (6) residence, and (7) mature age. It is imperative to discuss each of these grounds in detail because where they are proven by the petitioner, they attract a specific remedy under section 212 or 215 of the OLNLGE.

Undue Influence

The concept of undue influence is encapsulated under section 215(1) of the OLNLGE. The definition of undue influence is provided by s 102 of the *Criminal Code Act* (Ch 262). Section 102 states:

A person who

(a) uses or threatens to use any force or restrain or does or threatens to do any temporal or spiritual injury, or causes or threatens to cause any detriment of any kind to an elector:
   (i) in order to induce him to vote or refrain from voting at an election; or
   (ii) refrain from voting at an election on account of his having voted or refrain from voting at an election or,

(b) by force or fraud prevents or obstructs the free exercise of the franchise by an elector or by any such means compels or induces an elector to vote or election is guilty of the offence.

This provision makes undue influence a criminal offence which attracts a criminal liability. This position was made clear by the National Court in *State v Manasseh* [1978] PNGLR 119. In that case, the accused who was a Member of Parliament, convened a short meeting before the 1977 National Election and told the people that if they did not vote for him, they would be fined and imprisoned. The court found that the accused was guilty of attempted undue influence and convicted the Member accordingly. It is instructive to note that the court has to be satisfied beyond a reasonable doubt that the elements of undue influence are established before it can convict a person.

The elements of undue influence as set out in *State v Manasseh* are that the:

- accused told a person that he would be fined for not voting for the accused;
- statement was untrue or false;
- accused knew that the statement was false at the time it was made;
- statement could obstruct the free exercise of the franchise;
- accused intended such an obstruction;
- free exercise of the franchise was obstructed; and
- person obstructed was a voter.

The State has to prove that these elements exist to convince the court to convict the accused. On the evidence, the State did not establish that any person threatened was a voter, nor that any person was in fact obstructed in the free exercise of the franchise. The State also failed to establish the linkage between the elements of section 102 of the *Criminal Code* and undue influence for the purpose of section 215(1) of the OLNE. The State did, however, prove the elements of attempted undue influence and thus, the accused was found guilty and convicted by the court.[20]

In an election petition if the allegation of undue influence or an attempted undue influence is proven, the court will declare an election result null and void according to the stipulation of section 215(1)[21] of the OLNLGE.[22] In *Andrew Wabiria v Payable Elo* [1977] PNGLR 328, it was alleged that the successful candidate had unduly influenced the voters by telling them to vote for him or else they would be fined or goaled. The petitioner sought an order that the election be declared void in line with section 215(1) of the OLNE. The court found that the threats made by the respondent constituted a deliberate attempt to unduly influence the election and therefore, declared the election void.

Has the position changed with the enactment of the OLNLGE? The answer is simple. There are no changes. The concept is still the same under the OLNLGE. This position was confirmed by the Supreme Court in *Aita Ivarato v Peti Lafamana and the Electoral Commission* (1998) SC 563. However, the act of undue influence has taken on new and frightening forms. It has been observed that unlike in the past where elections were approached in a subtle and disciplined manner, people are now moving towards a gunpoint democracy.[23] The use of guns to force people to vote someone against their choice has become obvious.[24] For instance, in 1991, a year before the 1992 election, an intending candidate was caught by the police with 600 live bullets in his possession. When interrogated by the police, he informed them that he intended to use the bullets to force people to vote for him.[25]

The presence of illegal weapons in the elections adversely affects the free exercise of a person's right to vote guaranteed by the *Constitution*. The freedom guaranteed by section 50 of the *Constitution* to every citizen is difficult to exercise in a society where lethal weapons are openly used during elections. The use of guns at the national elections is a serious concern not only for the courts and every ordinary citizen, but also for the government. This prompted the government to call out the Defence Force soldiers for the first time in an election to provide security to the voters and polling officials in the 1997 National Election. The courts have indicated that they will not tolerate the intimidation and harassment of voters at the elections. This stand was made by the Supreme Court in *Aita Ivarato v Peti Lafamana* (supra) where the court said:

> Section 215(1) of the Organic Law gives full recognition to the underlying law principle that the parliamentary elections must be free. The people must be free to exercise their vote without fear or intimidation. So essential is this principle regarded that even a single instance of such a corrupt practice, as bribery or undue influence, if committed by a successful candidate, requires the election to be declared void.

However, the courts will not entertain allegations of bribery and undue influence which are committed after the voters had cast their votes. This distinction was made by the National Court in *Parry Zeipi v Gabia Gagarimabu* and endorsed by the Supreme Court in *Parry Zeipi v Gabia Gagarimabu* (SCR 5 of 1998).

Bribery

The next factor that gives rise to an election petition is bribery. The act of bribery has been defined as:

> A person is guilty of a corrupt practice if he is guilty of bribery. A person is guilty of bribery if directly or indirectly by himself or any other person on his behalf:

1. gives any money or procures any office to or for any voter or for any other person on behalf of any voter or to or for any other person induce any voter to vote or refrain from voting, or
2. corruptly does any such act as aforesaid on any voter having voted or refrain from voting, or
3. make any such gifts or procurements as aforesaid to or for any person in order to induce that person to procure, or endeavour to procure, the return of any person at an election or the vote of any voter; or
4. if upon, or in consequence of, any such gift or procurement as aforesaid, he procures or engages, promises or endeavours to procure the return of any person at an election or the vote of any voter.[26]

Bribery involves the act of giving someone (in this case a potential voter) some item of value in order to induce or influence his conduct in voting for the candidate or refrain from voting for another candidate. The acceptance of bribes is also an offence under s 103 of the *Criminal Code*. It has been said that:

> A voter is guilty of bribery if before or during an election, he directly or indirectly by himself or any other person on his behalf receives, agrees or contracts for any money, gift, loan on valuable conditions, office, place or employment for himself or for any other person for voting or agreeing to vote or for refraining or agreeing to refrain from voting.[27]

The act of bribery is a common allegation and usually quite difficult to prove. In an election dispute where bribery is raised as a ground, the court requires the petitioner to prove on the balance of probabilities that the allegation is true. The case of *Kaguel Koroka v Thomas Negints* (1982) N390 is relevant. In that case, the petitioner alleged that the winning candidate supplied food and provided entertainment to electoral officials to obtain their favour which influenced the electoral official to commit several errors and omissions resulting in the loss of a ballot box by the Electoral Commission containing 933 votes. The petitioner, however, failed to prove the nexus between the act complained of and the act of bribery and therefore, lost the case. A similar allegation was also raised in *Goasa Damena v Tony Siaguru* (1983) MP 150 of 1982. The petitioner in this case also lost the petition because he could not prove the act of bribery.

The offence of bribery is located in section 215(1) of the OLNLGE. This provision provides that where bribery or attempted bribery is proven in an election dispute, the election will be declared void. Where the allegation of bribery is not established, the court will not fetter with the election result. In the case of *Karo v Kidu* [1997] PNGLR 28, the petitioner alleged that there was bribery involved and the election of the respondent should be nullified pursuant to section 215(1) of the OLNLGE. The court held that there could have been an act of bribery involved in the case, but if the petition was to succeed detailed particulars of the allegation should have been spelt out to meet the requirement of section 208(a) of the OLNLGE. In this instance, the petitioner failed to satisfy the above requirement and therefore, the petition was dismissed.

It is instructive to note here that the act of bribery complained of must have influenced the voter and not any other person to vote or refrain from voting in the election. This distinction was made in *Desmond Baira v Kilroy Genia and Electoral Commission* (1998) SC 579. In this case the petitioner alleged and it was proven that the first respondent gave K1500 to one Aron Baro to nominate for the same seat occupied by the first respondent with a view to splitting the votes of the petitioner (as Baro and the petitioner were cousins). However, the petitioner failed to establish that: (1) Aron Baro was a voter, and (2) that because he was given the money he was induced not to vote or refrained from voting for the petitioner.

It is established law that where the act of bribery, if proven, was committed by the supporters of the winning candidate without his or her knowledge or without his or her authorization the findings will not affect the outcome of the election.[28] This is a common law principle which has been adopted by the PNG legal system.[29]

Illegal Conduct by Voters

A petitioner may rely on illegal conduct by voters as a ground to invalidate an election. This ground is usually raised against the supporters of the winning candidate. The conduct complained of takes various forms. This includes destruction of ballot boxes;[30] double voting;[31] inducement of polling officials;[32] threatening of voters through the use of dangerous weapons and tribal fights by supporters of opposing candidates. These events if proven can vitiate an election result.

Treating

This is an offence created by section 101 of the *Criminal Code*. This provision prohibits the candidates from providing food, drink, shelter, entertainment or any form of assistance to the electoral officials. This restriction also applies to a candidate's agent. Section 101 also makes it an offence for providing similar treatment to potential voters.

The case of *Thomas Kavali v James Kupul* (1982) MP 115 of 1982 is on point. The petitioner alleged that the respondent who had supplied a large amount of beer to some prospective voters acted in breach of section 101 of the *Criminal Code.* It was established that a large amount of beer was given to some potential voters. The court, however, ruled that although the fact was proven, the petitioner failed to prove that there was corruption involved. The court held that to establish treating under section 101, the petitioner must prove an element of corruption for him or her to succeed.

Procedural Irregularities by Electoral Officials

The next factor that gives rise to an election petition is procedural irregularities by electoral officials in the course of carrying out their duties assigned to them by the Electoral Commissioner. Because these errors or omissions are committed by electoral officials, the Electoral Commission invariably becomes a party in the proceedings. In other words, the Electoral Commission is liable for the procedural irregularities of its officers. According to section 215(3) of the OLNLGE, if in the view of the court, the electoral irregularities are likely to affect the outcome of an election, the election must be declared void. Electoral irregularities may take various forms. For instance, in the case of *Nahau Rooney v James Pokasui and Electoral Commission* [1982] PNGLR 496, the electoral officer did not know what to do with the informal votes because he was unsure of the rules relating to informal votes. In this case there was only one vote difference between the winning candidate and the petitioner. A total of 377 votes were declared informal.

The court ordered a recount and found that the petitioner was duly elected with a further 23 votes while the respondent polled only 7 votes. The court declared that the first respondent was not duly elected and further declared that the petitioner was duly elected.

In *Mokwa Mamando v Pyange Ni* [1977] PNGLR 496, the presiding officer failed to initial the back of the ballot papers, issue new ballot papers to replace defective ones and authenticate informal votes, all contrary to sections 126(2), 145 and 153 of the OLNE. The court exercised its powers under section 215(3) and declared the election void and ordered a new election.

And in the case of *Thomas Sumuno v Louis Ambane and Electoral Commission* (1998) N1718, the electoral officials, without the consent of the Electoral Commissioner, authorized the use of certain patrol boxes for the elections. The issue before the court was whether to count a total of 1,569 votes contained in the unauthorized patrol boxes. The court held that the votes should not be counted as valid as they were in unofficial boxes. However, for the purpose of determining whether the 1569 votes could have affected the election result as envisaged by section 215(3) the court proceeded to count the votes. When these votes were counted, the petitioner had 200 more votes than the respondent and if the ballot papers had been contained in authorised ballot boxes the petitioner could have won the election. The court ruled that these 1569 votes would have affected the election result and thus, declared the election of the respondent invalid and ordered a by-election. The ruling of the National Court was upheld in *Louis Ambane and Electoral Commission v Thomas Sumuno* (1998) SC 559.

A similar argument was raised in *Yuntivi Bao v Baki Reipa and Electoral Commission* (EP 32 of 1997). In this instance, the electoral officials were careless and did not protect the ballot boxes for the electorate and as a result the ballot boxes were stolen by some criminal elements and destroyed. The National Court upheld the petition and ordered a by-election for the electorate. The two respondents sought a review in the Supreme Court in *Baki Reipa and Electoral Commission v Yuntivi Bao* (1999) SC 606. However, the review was dismissed by the Supreme Court.

In yet another case, similar arguments were raised in *Charles Maino v Moi Avei and Electoral Commission* (2000), SC 633. The petitioner had argued that due to the misinformation given to some of the villages in his stronghold by the officials of the Electoral Commission, his supporters did not exercise their right and did not vote for him. Amet CJ who was presiding over the case held that although the electoral officials did commit electoral irregularities, the result of the election could not have been affected by these omissions.

It is clear that where the actions and omissions of the electoral officials will affect the outcome of the election results, the election will be declared void pursuant to section 215(3) of the OLNLGE. However, where the electoral irregularities will not affect the results the courts will not interfere with the election result.

Residence

The term *residence* refers to a place where an individual lives. Residence is an important pre-requisite in the electoral process. The concept itself is provided under section 103(2) of the *Constitution*.[33] An intending candidate must satisfy this requirement before he or she can be eligible to stand for election in an electorate. Section 103(2) (as amended) is in the following terms:

> A candidate for election to the Parliament must have been born in the electorate for which he intends to nominate or have resided in the electorate for a continuous period of two years immediately preceding his nomination or for a period of five years at any time and pay a deposit of K1000.00.

There are three elements of this provision. For a candidate to be eligible to stand in an electorate he or she must:

- have been born in the electorate for which he intends to nominate; or
- have resided in the electorate for a continuous period of two years preceding his nomination; or
- have lived for a period of five years at any time.

If a candidate does meet any of these three requirements, and in the event that he or she wins the election, his or her election can be declared void under section 212(1)(h) of the OLNLGE for failing to meet the requirements of section 103(2) of the *Constitution*. The issue of residence was carefully considered by the court in *Goasa Damena v Patterson Lowa* [1977] PNGLR 448. In that case the petitioner alleged that the winning candidate did not have the necessary residential qualifications required by section 103(2) of the *Constitution*. The respondent argued that he did own a house in the electorate (which he rented out to tenants) and as such he was eligible to contest the elections in the electorate. The court held that the respondent debarred himself from residing in the house by granting a tenancy. He was therefore, disqualified to be nominated as a candidate and elected as a Member of Parliament for the electorate.

There are two points about residence that need to be clarified at this juncture. The first point relates to the notion of "constructive residence". And the second relates to "actual residence". A person has "constructive residence" if he or she is a resident at an address even though he or she is temporarily absent from it. In this situation, the person must have the intention of returning at liberty to the address. Where he or she does not intend to return to the address, his or her residence is interrupted and he or she is no longer eligible to claim any rights in the place of residence.

The idea of constructive residence was discussed in *Kevin Masive v Iambakey Okuk* [1984] PNGLR 390. In that case, the petitioner challenged the validity of the respondent's election arguing that he did not qualify under section 103(2) of the *Constitution*. The respondent countered that he had a home and visited that home at regular intervals. His Honour, Amet J (as he then was) said that the doctrine of constructive residence was not appropriate at that time. The court held that the term reside in section 103(2) should be construed to mean to have physically lived permanently for a considerable period of time. The election of Okuk was therefore, declared null and void.

The same issue was raised in *Ludwig Schulge v Arthur Somare* (1997) N1798. In that case, the petitioner alleged that the respondent was not residentially qualified because he had never lived in the electorate at any one time. However, the respondent said that he had taken residence at a logging campsite for almost two years prior to the 1997 Elections and was therefore, eligible to nominate for the Open Electorate. The court held that the respondent's two years residence at the logging camp in the electorate was sufficient enough for the purpose of section 103(2) of the *Constitution* and dismissed the petition.

Also in *Ikupu v Mekere Mourata and Electoral Commission*, EP 19 of 1997, the petitioner challenged the validity of Sir Morauta's election on the ground that he was not residentially qualified to nominate for the Moresby North West Electorate because he did not live in the electorate. Sir Mourata responded by saying that he was a full-time student at the University of Papua New Guinea and sometimes lived at Tokarara which was within the electorate. The court accepted the respondent's argument and dismissed the petition.

In terms of "actual residence" the person must show that he or she has a home or an apartment where he or she lives in. Merely sleeping on the premises is not conclusive of residence. There must be actual and physical presence in order for one to be residentially qualified. It is also more than just constructive residence.[34]

Mature Age

Section 103(1) of the *Constitution* requires that a candidate must be more than 25 years of age to be eligible to nominate in an election. A person under the age of 25 years is not eligible to stand for elections in PNG. The first reported case on this issue was the case of *Okuk v Nikara* [1983] PNGLR 28. In that case, the petitioner alleged that the third runner up in the election was disqualified to stand for elections because he was not 25 years of age at the time of the elections. The petitioner contended that the votes collected by the under-aged candidate could have been distributed among others and himself, which would have impacted on the outcome of the election result. This placed the court in a very difficult position as it could not speculate on who should have collected those votes polled by the under-aged candidate. It therefore, dismissed the petition.

In the case of *Simon Kaumi v Akoka Doi* (1978) MP85 of 1977, the petitioner also alleged that the successful candidate was less than 25 years old when he nominated and got elected. The respondent provided evidence that showed that he was over 25 years old when he stood for elections. The court agreed with the respondent and dismissed the petition.

The foregoing discussions highlight the various issues that a petitioner has to carefully consider before he or she can institute a petition under the OLNLGE. The petitioner is required to set out in simple terms the specific details of every allegations that he or she intends to depend on to succeed in the petition. It is not the role of the court to assist petitioners by patching incomplete or purported petitions. The court plays a neutral role between the petitioner and the member elected. It is the job of the petitioner to rectify his or her petition by ensuring that all the limbs of section 208 are complied with.

Review of Election Petitions by the Supreme Court

The OLNLGE makes it very clear in section 220 that the decision of the National Court is final and is not subject to appeal. There can, therefore, be no appeal to the Supreme Court from a decision of the Court of Disputed Returns (National Court). Does this mean that the power of the Supreme Court to supervise the actions of the National Court is ousted by this provision? Obviously this cannot be the law given the inherent power of the Supreme Court to review all judicial acts of the National Court stipulated by section 155(2)(b) of the *Constitution*.

Section 155(2)(b) of the *Constitution* empowers the Supreme Court to scrutinize the judicial activities of the National Court. There is a long line of authorities which have enlarged this power of the Supreme Court to cover the review of election petition cases. These include: *Balakau v Torato* [1983] PNGLR 242; *Application by Kassap and Yama* [1988-89] PNGLR 197; *Electoral Commission and Henry Smith v Bire Kimisopa* (SCR 93 of 1997); *Daniel Kapi v Takai Kapi and Electoral Commission* (1998) SC 548; *Michael Nali v Stephen Mendepo and Electoral Commission* (1998) SC 542 and *Korak Yasona v Castan Maibawa and Electoral Commission* (SCR 81 of 1998).

This power has been successfully invoked by aggrieved parties to review the decision of the National Court, thereby bypassing section 220 of the OLNLGE. The exercise of this power by the Supreme Court has, however, been sporadic because of the absence of any formal rules to regulate the review of election petitions. This ad hoc approach has created confusion for the petitioners and their counsels and has led to the confusion in the law. In *Parry Zeipi v Gabia Gagarimabu and Electoral Commission* (SCR 5 of 1998) the Supreme Court was very critical of the abuse of its power under section 155(2)(b) by aggrieved parties. It said:

> The indiscriminate use of the judicial review process under the *Constitution* section 155(2)(b) as an alternative appeal mechanism must be strongly discouraged,

particularly so in election petition cases where parties have three or more bites at the cherry. This was never intended to be that way at all,...

The law is now settled that the provisions of the *Supreme Court Act* and the *Supreme Court Rules* do not apply to reviews made pursuant to s 155(2)(b). In *Dick Mune v Pail Poto* (1996) SC 499 and *Viviso Seravo and Electoral Commission v John Giheno* (1998) SC 539, the Supreme Court held that the provisions of the Act do not apply to judicial review under section 155 (2)(b). And in *Korak Yasona v Castan Maibawa and Electoral Commission* (1998) SC 552 and *Mathias Ijape v Henry Smith and Electoral Commission* (SCR 92 of 1997) the Supreme Court ruled that the provisions of the *Supreme Court Rules* cannot be applied to oust the right of a person to invoke the power of the Supreme Court under section 155(2)(b).

Elections for Local-level Governments

Local-level governments are the creatures of the *Organic Law on Provincial Government and Local-level Government* (OLPGLLG). They are created together with provincial governments by section 5 of the OLPGLLG. They are given legal personality by section 6 of the Organic Law. Local-level governments can, therefore, sue and be sued. They can also own and dispose of property.

Local-level governments comprise a president and ward councillors who are elected according to the process defined under Part XIX of the OLNLGE. The presidents of the local-level governments in a province and the relevant Open Members of Parliament of the province and the Provincial or Regional Member of Parliament comprise the provincial government.[35] There is, therefore, no separate elections for membership of provincial governments.

Prior to the enactment of the OLNLGE, the conduct of local government elections was governed by the *Local Government Act*. The local elections were conducted by District Administrators. The Act was, however, not very popular with the voters at the local level. The enactment of the OLNLGE has divested the Electoral Commission with the responsibility of administering all local-level government elections. The Organic Law imposes a duty on the Electoral Commission to go directly to the electorates and conduct local-level government elections. According to section 280 of the Organic Law, the conduct of elections for the national and local-level government must be held simultaneously.

The supervision and administration of local-level government elections are conducted on behalf of the Electoral Commission by Returning Officers appointed under section 236 of the Organic Law. This provision states that the same Returning Officers appointed for the parliamentary elections will also be the Returning Officers for local-level government elections. Section 242 of the OLNLGE permits the use of the same Common Roll used in the elections for the Open Electorates for local-level government elections.

The writs for local-level government elections are to be issued by the Minister for Provincial and Local Government Affairs acting in accordance with the advice of the Electoral Commissioner. Nominations for local-level governments are to be made in accordance with section 281 of the Organic Law. The polling period for local-level government elections should be not more than 11 weeks. A number of actions which are deemed as illegal practices in local-level government elections are enumerated under section 286 of the OLNLGE.

The stipulations of the Organic Law on the process and method of conducting local-level government elections are less cumbersome and limited in number than those for the national elections. This point becomes clear when the provisions relating to the two different levels of elections are compared. There are only 88[36] provisions relating to local-level government elections. This number is more than double for the national elections as there are 233 provisions dealing with the national elections.

Election Petitions for the Local-level Government Elections

Local-level government election petitions are instituted under section 287 of the OLNLGE. This provision contains a number of directives which require clarification. It is imperative that the provision is set out in full. Section 288 is in the following terms:

1. Subject to this section, the provisions of Part XVIII of this law other than sections 208(e), 209, 210, 212(2) and 213, shall apply as the provisions of this law relating to disputed Local-level Government elections and returns.
2. References in Part XVIII to–
   (a) "Clerk of Parliament" shall be read as to "Clerk of the Local-level Government"; and
   (b) "electorate" shall be read as to a "ward"; and
   (c) "member" shall be read as to a "member of the Local-level Government"; and
   (d) "National Court" shall read as to a "District Court"; and
   (e) "Registrar of National Court" shall be read as to Clerk of the District Court; and
   (f) "Speaker" shall be read as to the "Head of the Local-level Government".
3. A petition to dispute an election or return shall be filed at the District Court in the town in which are situated the headquarters of the Provincial Government of the Province which includes the area of the Local-level

Government in respect of which the election was held.

4. At the time of filing the petition the petitioner shall deposit with the Clerk of the District Court the sum of K50 as a security for costs.
5. Proceedings shall not be had on a petition unless the requirements of subsections (3) and (4), section 208(a) to (d) inclusive are complied with.

An election petition disputing a local-level government election must be filed at the District Court in the provincial capital. And the petition must be accompanied by a deposit of K50 as security for cost with the Clerk of Court at the District Court. Given the structure of section 287, election petitions in the District Court must:

- set out the facts relied on to invalidate the election or return; and
- specify the relief to which the petitioner claims entitled; and
- be signed by a candidate at the election in dispute or by a person who was qualified to vote at the election; and
- be attested by two witnesses whose occupations and address are stated.

It has been mentioned above that the National Court is mandated to strike out any petition that does not comply with the requirements of section 208 of the OLNLGE. According to section 287, the District Court is also required to scrutinise an election petition to ensure that it complies with section 208. Section 287(5) makes it mandatory for the District Court to strike out any election petition that does not comply with the requirements under section 208(a) to (d).[37]

It is clear from the reading of this provision that the election petition process for local-level governments does not deviate much from that of the national elections. Apart from the changes in institutions and personnel, the law remains much the same for election disputes at the local level. Given the stringent controls applied by the National Court and the Supreme Court in election petition cases, it remains to be seen whether the District Courts will apply the same level of control in their jurisdiction.

In the case of *Ted Diro v Opa Taureka & Or* (OS No 93 of 2000) Mr Diro, who is the Regional Member for Central Province applied to the court to declare the elections of Opa Taureka and Peter Kara as president of Aroma and Rigo Coast Rural Local-level Government void respectively. The aim of the application was to enable Mr Diro to assume his position as Governor of the Central Province which he lost to Opa Taureka. Diro also applied to the court to restrain the two presidents from acting or holding themselves out as presidents of these local-level governments and from attending the Central Provincial Assembly meetings. Diro argued that the two presidents were elected at a time when the two local-level governments did not have any valid standing orders as required by section 18 of the *Local-level Governments Administration Act* 1997. Because of this defect, the applicant argued that the elections of the two presidents were of no effect and thus, void. The court ruled that:

- to grant such a declaration would be contrary to the plain intentions of the OLNLGE.
- to declare a breach of a law on the error disclosed, the court would be enforcing an impossibility, again not the intention of Parliament. It is reasonable that the court could in such circumstance interpret the mode of election and the promulgation of standing orders as directory than mandatory.
- because section 74 of the *Local-level Government's Administration Act* provides for the validation of all functions, duties, responsibilities and exercise of power

> by local-level government substantially in compliance with the provisions of this Act during the relevant period and because the determination of whether there has been substantial compliance resides in the Minister. It is not necessary or appropriate that this court make any declaration at this time.

The court, therefore, declined the application.

Jurisdiction of the Court

Local-level government election petitions are addressed to the District Courts. The District Courts exercise the same powers as the National Court when dealing with election petitions. They are also empowered by section 287 to deliver the same kind of remedies as the National Court.

Legal Representation

Lawyers can make an appearance for the disputants in an election petition so long as their appearance complies with section 222 of the OLNLGE. And because of the directive under section 287, the same arguments that were raised for lawyers in the National Court equally applies here.

Legal Costs

In relation to costs, the District Court functions more like the National Court because of the stipulations of section 287. That is, the District Court can award costs against an unsuccessful petitioner. The award of legal costs is permitted by section 223 of the OLNLGE. Section 223 states that the National Court may award costs against an unsuccessful party to a petition. In the event that the petition is for a local-level government election, the words "National Court" used here can be read to mean the District Court. Hence, the District Court that can award costs against the unsuccessful party in an election petition.

Conclusion

Elections have become a very intense and expensive exercise for both the government and the people. Since the first formal election in 1964, the electoral process has also become more complicated and electioneering by candidates and their supporters has become very sophisticated.

In 1991, a journalist reported that elections have become more violent because of the use of guns.[38] A similar observation was also made by the Electoral Commissioner at that time. The Electoral Commissioner reported that:

> We are now facing more citizens of better education and agitation abilities than five years ago, more readily made lethal weapons and more candidates. The competition for prestige and political power will this time as I gather from research and other intelligence information be more intense than ever before.[39]

The likelihood of these kinds of corrupt and illegal practices finding their way into the court rooms by way of election petitions is very probable. Given this scenario, most of the issues that have been raised by the authors are very pressing and require urgent action to facilitate the upsurge in election petitions. Any delay in reforming the election review process will result in the flooding of the courts by losing candidates and the unnecessary flurry of review applications before the Supreme Court. It is imperative that the courts also take a very proactive approach to resolving some of these issues so that in the wider context the disputants, the constituencies, and the public are satisfied with the outcome of their votes.

Notes

* Eric Kwa was the former Executive Dean of the School of Law at the University of Papua New Guinea. He is

currently a PhD scholar at the Faculty of Law of the University of Auckland, New Zealand. Mr. Wilfred Golman is a Lecturer at the Law School of the University of Papua New Guinea. We want to record our special thanks to Mr. Daniel Kop of Patterson Lawyers in Port Moresby, Papua New Guinea, for giving us permission to use some parts of his work generally in this paper.

1. The origin of the CPC and its work is discussed by Eric Kwa in Kwa, EL, *Constitutional Law of Papua New Guinea* (Sydney: Law Book Company Ltd, 2001). See also Regan, A, Jessep, O and Kwa, EL (ed), *Twenty Years of the Papua New Guinea Constitution* (Sydney: Law Book Company Ltd, 2001).
2. Section 125 provides for the Electoral Boundaries Commission whose main function is to determine electoral boundaries. The Electoral Boundaries Commission is established by Part III of the OLNLGE.
3. This responsibility is mandated by s 16 of the OLNLGE.
4. See the article by Frank Senge in the PNG daily paper the *Post Courier*, 25 November, 1991.
5. For instance, polling was delayed from May to June 1997 as a result of the Electoral Commission's difficulties in compiling the rolls. See also Hegarty, D, *Politics in PNG: Studies on the 1977 National Elections* (Port Moresby: UPNG Press, 1982), 5.
6. Ketan, J and Mangi, J, *Assessment of PNG Electoral System (Vol 1) Gazelle Open Election* (Port Moresby: NRI Discussion Paper, 1991).
7. *Louis Ambane and Electoral Commission v Thomas Sumono* (1998), SC 559.
8. *The Post Courier*, 31 May, 2000.
9. Ibid.
10. The summary of the findings of the Group was published by the second daily newspaper of PNG, *The National*, 2 July, 2000.
11. See the discussion of this limb of section 208 by Justice Injia in *Sir Julius Chan v Ephraim Apelis and the Electoral Commission* (1997) N1627. The decision by Injia was however, overturned in *Application by Julius Chan* (SCR 71 of 1997).

12. *Biri v Ninkama* [1982] PNGLR 342 at p. 345.
13. *Electoral Commission and Henry Smith v Bire Kimisopa* (SCR 3 of 1997).
14. See also *Billy Jababa v Iambakey Okuk* [1983] PNGLR 69. In this case the National Court had to consider before an election but after the nomination whether Mr. Okuk was eligible to nominate for the Ungai Bena Open Electorate. Mr. Okuk was enrolled in the Kundiawa Electorate but sought to nominate for the Ungai Bena Electorate one day before the nomination period closed. The Returning Officer refused to accept his nomination because of section 85(2)(b)(iii) of the OLNE. This provision requires that nomination by a person enrolled in another electorate must be made more than seven days before the nomination period expires. In this case, this particular provision was not complied with and thus, the court said the nomination was invalid.
15. See *Martin Thompson v Pokasui and the Electoral Commission* [1988] PNGLR 210.
16. Personal communication with Sir Julius Chan in 2000. In fact one of the reasons why Sir Julius Chan's case against Ephraim Apelis was thrown out in November 2001 was because he did not pay in full the amount ordered by the Supreme Court as security for costs.
17. See also *Melchoir Pep v Puri Riyong and Electoral Commission* (1999) SC 614. This case was dismissed for want of prosecution. However, the non-payment of K51,000.00 in security for costs by the petitioner also played a part in the dismissal of the petition.
18. *Michael Nali v Stephen Mendepo and Electoral Commission* (1998), SC 542.
19. EP. No. 49 of 1997. The petitioner alleged that there was bribery and errors or omissions and sought in the petition to declare the West New Britain election in 1997 absolutely void. The court found that the petitioner failed to comply with the requirements of the first and the second limbs of section 208 and consequently dismissed the petition.
20. See also *Malipu Balakau v Paul Torato* (1983) MP 132 of 1982.

21. See the ruling on remedies under s 215(1) made by the Supreme Court in *Korak Yasona v Castan Maibawa and Electoral Commission* (1998), SC 552.
22. *Nerville Bourne v Manasseh Voeto* [1977] PNGLR 298.
23. Standish, B, *1992 PNG Election* (Canberra: ANU Press, 1996).
24. *The Post Courier*, 25 October, 1991.
25. *The Post Courier*, 21 October, 1991.
26. *Halsbury's Laws of England* (4th Ed). Vol. 15 p. 527.
27. Id, at p. 533.
28. See *Yano Belo v Soso Temu* (1983) MP 118 of 1982; *Richard Moaitz v Tom Awasa: Re Huon Gulf Open Parliamentary Election*, (1983), N424 and *Komane Wasege v Mathias Karani* (1998), N1696.
29. According to *Halsbury's Laws of England*, above n. 26: "A candidate is not liable, nor his election to be avoided for any illegal practice relating to false statements committed by his agent or other than election agents unless; (1) it can be shown that the candidate or his election agent has authorized or consented to the committing of illegal practice by the other agent or has paid for the circulation of the false statement constituting the illegal practice, or (2) an election court finds and reports that the candidate's election was procured or materially assisted in consequence of the making or publishing of such false statement.
30. *Tindiwi v The Electoral Commission, Sauk and Wasun* [1987] PNGLR 128.
31. Double voting is an offence under section 191 of the OLNLGE. It is also a criminal offence under section 100 of the *Criminal Code*. The discussion by Ketan and Mangi provide a clear example; above, n. 6.
32. *Kaguel Koroka v Thomas Negints* (1982), N 390.
33. There is an Organic Law called the *Organic Law on Residence*. This Organic Law is purposely for determining the eligibility for PNG citizenship.
34. *Bouraga v Berghuser* [1982] PNGLR 381.
35. For a detailed discussion about the provincial governments and local-level governments see Kwa, above, n1 at p130 and Ghai, Y and Regan A, "Decentralisation:

1976-1995" in Regan, A, Jessep, O and Kwa, E (ed), above, n. 1, at p. 161.

36. This figure is taken from Part XVIII and Part XIX.
37. This provision actually collapses and amalgamates the requirements of sections 209 and 210 of the OLNLGE. It would seem that the exclusion by subsection (1) of the same section is immaterial.
38. Frank Senge, above, n. 4.
39. *The Post Courier*, 1 November, 1991.

Chapter Three

Overview of 1997 Election Petitions

*Sir Arnold Amet, CBE, LLD**

Introduction

The *Organic Law on National and Local-level Government Elections* 1997 (OLNLGE)[1] bestows on every candidate at an election or any person qualified to vote at the election the right to challenge the validity of the election or return by presenting a petition to the National Court. The role of the National Court in hearing election disputes is to check both the personal and democratic credentials of those claiming a seat in the national Parliament and the local-level governments. Personal credentials involve qualifications as to age, residence and nomination, while democratic credentials relate to the integrity and propriety of the election.

Since independence, the tendency to challenge the returns of election in the court has been a regular feature of the PNG electoral process. This may be due to the level of corruption in the actual conduct of elections or the level of efficiency with which elections are operated. At the same time, it is also a response to the enormous power and prestige often at stake in an election.

The number of petitions that were filed after the 1997 Elections to the Parliament was phenomenally high. This obviously stretched the capacity and resources of the courts to the limit. Notwithstanding its unwavering commitment to the ideals of a just, speedy and inexpensive disposition of every petition, the National Court has not found it easy under this sustained pressure to operate according to these ideals.

Clearly, when the judicial system fails to dispose of election petitions expeditiously and efficiently, the parties rightly feel that they are receiving no justice at all. The delay in the disposition of election petitions is a matter of great concern not only to the parties, but to the general public as well, for an election petition is a means by which the integrity and credibility of the electoral system is maintained. It is thus in the public interest and fundamental to the functioning of our fragile democracy that contested election results be determined judiciously and with expedition.

This chapter presents an overview of the election petitions that were filed following the 1997 Elections. In particular, it provides a quantitative analysis of the facts and figures of the election petitions to illustrate their significant features. The analysis focuses on the common grounds that were alleged in all the petitions, the kind of legal issues that arose from the alleged grounds, and the factors that hindered the just and efficient disposition of the petitions. The chapter concludes by suggesting a set of recommendations aimed at improving the processing and disposition of election petitions in the future.[2]

Main Features of 1997 Election Petitions

The main features of the 1997 election petitions were:

- Litigation explosion;
- Multiple petitions against winning candidates;
- Multiplicity of Supreme Court reviews;
- Delay; and
- Low success rate.

Each of these issues are discussed separately in what follows.

Litigation Explosion

Under section 208 of the OLNLGE, a petition disputing the validity of an election may be filed within 40 days of the declaration of the result of the election. According to the National Court database on election petitions, at the close of the 40 days time limit for filing election petitions following the 1997 General Elections, 88 petitions were registered with the National Court. In a rare case, a further petition[3] was filed well after the elections in 1998, bringing the total[4] to 89. This figure represents an increase of 31 per cent over the total number of petitions (58) registered after the 1992 Elections. Five other petitions arising out of recounts ordered from the earlier petitions were later registered in 1999. The Electoral Commission was named as co-respondent in almost all these petitions and was, therefore, a party to all the election petitions.

Multiple Petitions against Winning Candidates

Although there were 89 election petitions, this does not necessarily mean that the election results of 89 electorates were challenged in court. One of the significant features of the 1997 election petitions was the multiple petitions that were brought against some of the winning candidates. As illustrated in Figure 1, Mr. Iangalio[5] alone had four different election petitions brought against him; Mr. Basua[6] and Fr. Ambane[7] each had three separate election petitions brought against them; while Sir Mekere Morauta,[8] Mr Taku,[9] Mr. Smith,[10] Mr. Miru,[11] Mr. Lafamana,[12] Mr Reipa,[13] Mr. Kapi[14] and Mr. Ipatas[15] each had two petitions filed against them. The total number of electorates whose election results were actually challenged is 70. This figure represents 64 per cent of the 109 electorates.

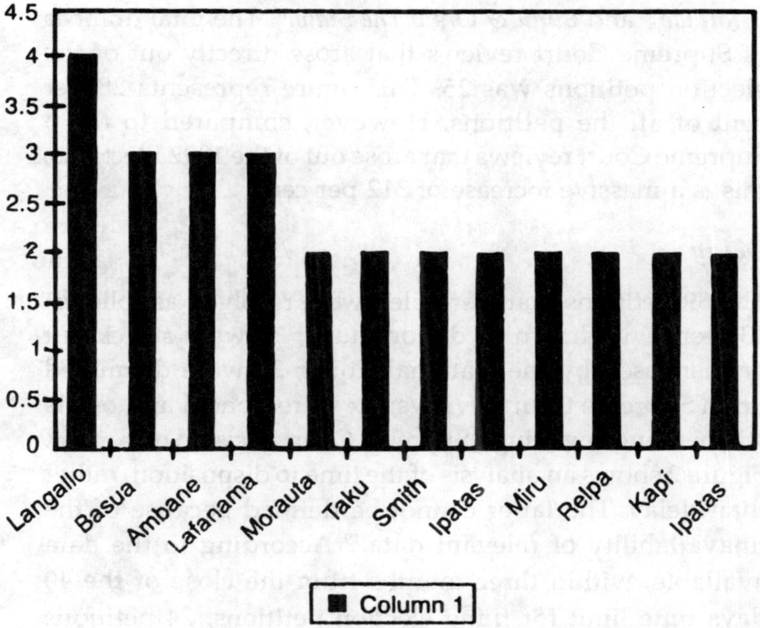

Figure 1: Members challenged in multiple petitions

Multiple Supreme Court Reviews

One of the most significant feature of the 1997 Election petitions was the dramatic increase in the number of Supreme Court reviews that were filed by either unsuccessful petitioners or sitting members who lost their seats as a result of an election petition. This development is a direct consequence of the Supreme Court's interpretation of its judicial review powers under section 155(2)(b) of the *Constitution* in *Avia Aihi v The State,*[16] *Balakau v Toratao*[17] and *Sunu & Ors v The State.*[18] The total number of Supreme Court reviews that arose directly out of the election petitions was 25. This figure represents 28 per cent of all the petitions. However, compared to the 8 Supreme Court reviews that arose out of the 1992 Elections, this is a massive increase of 312 per cent.

Delay

The 89 petitions that were filed were resolved as follows: 13 were withdrawn or discontinued; 36 were struck out or dismissed by the National Court; 33 were dismissed upon Supreme Court reviews; six were upheld and one is still pending, awaiting a Supreme Court decision on review. Figure 2 shows an analysis of the time to disposition, rather than delay. The latter cannot be defined because of the unavailability of relevant data.[19] According to the data available, within three months from the close of the 40 days time limit for filing election petitions, 24 petitions had been disposed of. Thereafter, 15 petitions were completed within six months from the date of filing, 23 were resolved within nine months from the date of filing, nine were disposed of within 12 months from the date of filing, 15 were resolved within 24 months and three were completed within 48 months or more.[20] It should be pointed out that within 12 months from the date of filing, the National Court had completed preliminary hearing of all the 89 petitions filed immediately after the elections. In other words, the petitions that took longer than 12 months to dispose of were those that were delayed by protracted Supreme Court hearings.

Time Taken to Dispose of Petitions

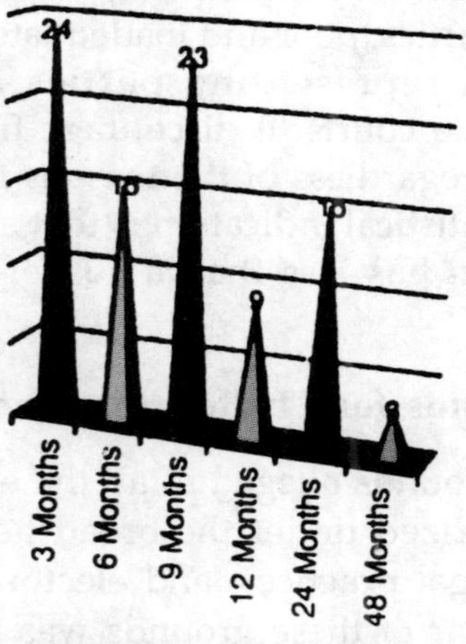

Figure 2: Time to Disposition

Low Success Rate

From the total number of election petitions filed only six petitions were upheld. And these were:

1. *Miru v Basua, Mango & EC (1998) SC 62, 79 and 92;*
2. *Sumono v Ambane & EC (1998) SC 559;*
3. *Tano v Reipa & EC;*
4. *Daniel Kapi v Takai Kapi (1998) SC 570;*
5. *Poyle v Papak & EC; and*
6. *Ivarato v Lafamana & EC (1998) SC 563.*

It is instructive to observe that the Supreme Court and not the National Court declared all these petitions successful. As a consequence of the success of these petitions, by-elections were held in the affected constituencies. Following the by-elections, two of the respondents regained their seats.

There were 89 election petitions filed after the 1997 Elections. Of this only 7 per cent of the petitions were successful (6) while 93 per cent were unsuccessful (83). The failure of election petitions may be due to fabrication of facts by the parties, poor and inadequate advocacy skills of the counsel representing parties or the general disposition of the courts to discourage frivolous suits. It is obvious that regardless of the reasons for the failure of petitions, the statistical indication is that a petitioner in an election petition has less than a 10 per cent chance of success.

Common Grounds for Challenging Election Petitions

The common grounds alleged in all the election petitions may be summarized under the broad headings of basic ineligibility, illegal practices, and electoral irregularities. The most popular of these grounds was illegal practices. It was pleaded in 76 petitions, representing 85 per cent of all the petitions. This was followed by electoral irregularities which was pleaded in 69 petitions, representing 77 per cent. Basic ineligibility came third and was pleaded in 6 petitions, a mere 6 per cent.

It is important to observe that, in spite of the fact that bribery or attempted bribery was alleged in 76 election petitions, not a single one of these allegations was successfully proven in court.

Legal Issues in the National Court

The critical legal issues that arose out of the determination of most election petitions in the National Court were as follows:

- Jurisdiction of the National Court;
- Disqualifications under section 103 of the Constitution;
- Filing of petition;
- Attestation of petition;
- Want of prosecution;

- Pleading of facts;
- Pleading of relief;
- Proof of illegal practices;
- Proof of electoral irregularities; and
- Remedies

The legal arguments underpinning these issues provide an accurate barometer for assessing not only the validity of the election results but also the overall effectiveness and efficiency of the electoral laws and processes. At the same time, the factual evidence in the petitions reveals the appalling instances of corruption that plague the electioneering process and the administrative and logistical problems faced by the Electoral Commission and its officials. In the following pages the samples of these issues raised in the National Court and the principles established by the court or, where relevant, by the Supreme Court, to resolve them will be discussed.

Legal Issues in the Supreme Court

The Supreme Court, as indicated above, dealt with many applications for judicial review under section 155(2)(b) of the *Constitution* relating to points of law. The substantive issues that the court ruled on in its review of the petitions were invariably interpretation of provisions of the *Constitution* or the Organic Law. In addition, there were numerous interlocutory applications to the court for a multitude of orders, which tended to prolong the proceedings sometimes unnecessarily. The resort to Supreme Court reviews has been justifiably criticized as a source of unwarranted cost, delay and inconvenience in the disposition of election petitions. But the positive side to these review applications is that they provided the Supreme Court with the opportunity to:

1. Interpret and clarify the provisions of the Constitution and the Organic Law;
2. Develop the law on the practice and procedure for judicial review applications brought under s 155(2)(b) of the Constitution; and
3. Further build upon the emerging jurisprudence of election petitions.

Some reference has already been made to the decisions of the Supreme Court on several legal issues that relate directly to election petitions. Some of those decisions pertaining specifically to the practice and procedure for judicial review applications brought under section 155(2)(b) of the *Constitution* will be highlighted in this section of the paper. Although these issues were determined in the course of the review of election petitions, they have a wider implication for the general judicial review jurisdiction of the Supreme Court. The issues covered by these decisions may be summarized under the following headings: (1) Jurisdiction of the Supreme Court; (2) Procedure for applying for judicial review under section 155(2)(b) of the *Constitution*; (3) Stay of proceedings; (4) Slip Rule applications; and (5) Security for costs.

Major Concerns

Politicians and the general public have been very critical of election petitions. Their concerns are not directed at the quality of decision-making, or at the integrity or professionalism of the judges and court staff. Instead, the criticism is levelled at the systemic intractable delay in case processing and resolution of the petitions. The major complaint is that election petitions take too long and cost litigants too much. Privately, even judges, court officers, and practitioners acknowledge that the court processes by which election petitions are resolved are far from satisfactory. In particular, there are too many Supreme Court reviews and many of these do not help to advance the matter to trial, or to resolve it.

Delay

The most pressing problem of election petitions is delay. Delay leads to injustice. The most important impact of delay in the disposition of election petitions is the denial of representation in Parliament and the uncertainty it causes in the representation of an electorate in the Parliament. As a consequence of this, an electorate may be deprived and denied of its rightful services like funds allocation, infrastructure development projects, aid funds and other necessary benefits from the government and other sources.

Delay also causes immense financial and psychological pressure on the parties. Indeed, prolonged election petitions add to hefty legal costs which invariably take their toll on the parties, the judicial system and the State.

Costs

There is no available information on the cost of election petitions to the judicial system. This is because no research has been conducted on the cost of judicial time and resources as a component of civil litigation costs. However, the cost of organizing recounts and conducting by-elections may be considered as costs to the State.

Supreme Court Reviews

There were too many Supreme Court reviews. The multiplicity of the Supreme Court reviews prolonged the hearings of most petitions unnecessarily and added up to the prohibitive legal costs.

Conclusion

The 2002 General Elections is just around the corner. The public expectation, especially of the politicians, is that, at least, some genuine effort will be made to improve the handling and disposition of election petitions. Based on our understanding of the complex and interrelated issues of cost, delay, efficiency and inappropriate legal procedures and tactics that affect the processing and disposition of election petitions, there is an urgent need for a fundamental change in the system of processing election petitions. The critical areas that require reform are the processing regime and the review process. The following recommendations will assist in addressing these areas.

1. *Policy on Delivery of Election Petition Judgments*

The National Court must formulate and adopt a general policy on the time standards for the disposition of election petitions and the delivery of election petition judgments. The standard should aim at hearing and disposing of all election petitions within six months from the date of filing.

2. *Expedited Proceedings*

In order to meet the standard proposed above, it will be necessary to introduce a pilot project and experiment with three judges who should be relieved from normal judicial workload and assigned exclusively to hearing election petitions. An ancillary part of this project should address the need to provide adequate support staff and resources to expedite the processing and disposition of the election petitions.

3. *Fast Track Procedure*

The current individual docket system (IDS) case management approach introduced by the National Court

Registry may be retained, with some refinement to make effective use of judicial time and expertise. In addition, a fast track procedure, comprising the following three stages, should be adopted: pre-trial conference—interlocutory applications—trial. The procedure for the conduct of pre-trial conferences should be standardized. The pre-trial conference order and the agreement on trial dates at the end of the pre-trial conference should be binding and no appeal should be allowed against them. The pre-trial conference order should be rigidly enforced. Once the trial begins, no interlocutory applications should be allowed. Similarly, once the National Court makes a final order at the end of the hearing, no appeal should be allowed against the decision.

The responsibility for discovery of documents and routine procedures must be assigned to the Registrar. The procedure for discoveries must be simplified and Registry staff should be trained to follow the fast-track procedure.

4. Banning Supreme Court Reviews

Election petition reviews must be removed from the judicial review jurisdiction of the Supreme Court under section 155(2)(b) of the *Constitution*. Although this may raise a controversial constitutional issue about the power of the Supreme Court, the court must be bold to take on the challenge and develop new rules and procedures designed specifically for election petition reviews.

The removal of election petitions from the judicial review jurisdiction of the Supreme Court will mean that National Court decisions on election petitions will become "final and conclusive and without appeal, and shall not be questioned in any way" as intended by section 220 of the OLNLGE.

5. *Practice Rules and Directions*

The current *Practice Directions* or *Presentation and Conduct of Election Petitions* (1997) maybe retained and updated to incorporate any practice and procedural changes that are adopted. A further step, worth considering, is to promulgate these Practice Directions into rules of the National Court in order to make them binding.

Notes

* Chief Justice of Papua New Guinea.

1. This Act replaced the former *Organic Law on the National Elections,* but it is almost identical to the Organic Law repealed by it. For the sake of convenience, the new legislation and the repealed statute will be referred to as "the Organic Law" and the numbering of the provisions will remain as in the original legislation.
2. The data sources for this part of this chapter include the National Court Registry case files, the Supreme Court Registry case files, the National Court database on election petitions and the Electoral Commission database on elections.
3. *Peipul v Niningi & EC* EP 01/98.
4. Sixteen of these petitions were filed by defeated members of the previous Parliament.
5. *Kaeok v Iangalio & EC* EP 13/97; *Arete v Iangalio & EC* EP 46/97; *Ranveta v Iangalio & EC* EP 65/97 and *Mark v Iangalio* EP 70/97.
6. *Miru v Basua, Mango & EC* EP 16/97; *Nakisi v Basua & EC* EP 26/97 and *Tulapi v Basua & EC* EP 55/97.
7. *Summuno v Ambane & EC* EP 40/97 and *Porr v Ambane & EC* EP 59/97 and *Mai v Ambane & EC* EP 67/97.
8. *Tongia v Morauta & EC* EP 18/97 and *Ikupu v Morauta & EC* EP 19/97.
9. *Unagi v Taku & EC* EP 06/97 and *Fernandez v Taku* EP 10/97.
10. *Kimisopa v Smith & EC* EP 11/97 and *Ijape v Smith & EC* EP 47/97.

11. *Basua v Miru & EC* EP 01/99 and *Tulapi v Miru & EC* EP 02/99.
12. *Ivarato v Lafanama & EC* EP 39/97 and *Gotha v Lafanama & EC* EP 03/99
13. *Bao v Reipa & EC* EP 32/97 and *Tanao v Reipa & EC* EP 41/97.
14. *Takai Kapi v Daniel Kapi & EC* EP 04/99 and *Aiyok v Daniel Kapi & EC* EP 05/99.
15. *Lambu v Ipatas & EC* EP 74/97 and *Pato v Ipatas & EC* EP 79/97.
16. [1981] PNGLR 81.
17. [1983] PNGLR 242.
18. [1984] PNGLR 305.
19. This analysis includes those petitions that were either withdrawn or discontinued because they were not withdrawn or discontinued immediately after filing. Many of them had gone through some stages of the hearing process in the National Court and some even had progressed to the Supreme Court before they were withdrawn or discontinued.
20. The total number of petitions accounted for in this analysis is 81. This is because information on the time to disposition for the remaining 8 is unavailable.

Part Two

Judicial Review of Election Petitions

Chapter Four

Judicial Responsibility in Securing a Fair and Just Election Result

*Sheehan, M J**

Election petitions as we know are the constitutional means for challenging the validity of elections for Parliament and local-level governments. The *Organic Law on National and Local Level Government Elections* (OLNLGE) provides the code for the conduct of elections and in determining the outcomes of petitions challenging such elections.

The mode of challenging elections to Parliament has not always been orderly. On 5th November, 1605 (396 years ago) a dissatisfied citizen in England set out to file and determine the election of members of Parliament by placing barrels of gunpowder under the House of Parliament. That informal challenge was firmly rejected by the authorities and Guy Fawkes was arrested. The order for costs in that case was very severe. He was beheaded.

Though the courts in Papua New Guinea have not really been as severe on unsuccessful petitioners as in the case of Guy Fawkes, the decisions of the National and Supreme Courts do show a strict interpretation of election laws. Also, the parties to such disputes have found that the cost of presentation of election petitions is very expensive.

Strict Interpretation of Election Petitions

The strict rules of interpretation in regards to election laws starts with the case of *Delba Biri v Bill Gimbogl Ninkama* [1982] PNGLR 342. The significance of this decision must be recognized to appreciate the subsequent decisions of the National and Supreme Courts relating to election petitions and judicial reviews of those petitions.

In that case the Supreme Court, in an unanimous decision, ruled that:

(a) An election petition must comply strictly with each and every requirement of section 208 of the Organic Law;
(b) National Court on hearing a petition may allow an amendment to the petition provided that the application for amendment is made within the time for filing of the election petition provided in the Organic Law;
(c) National Court shall not allow, and does not have the power to allow, an amendment of a petition *after the period allowed* for the filing of the petition by the Organic Law.

Election petitions start with section 208 of the Organic Law and thus, it is appropriate to set out the essentials of this section in full. Section 208 states that:

A petition shall:

(a) set out the facts relied on to invalidate the election or return;
(b) specify the relief to which the petitioner claims to be entitled;
(c) be signed by a candidate in the election in dispute or by a person who was qualified to vote at the election;
(d) be attested by two witnesses whose occupation and address are stated; and

(e) be filed in the Registry of the National Court at Port Moresby or at the court house in any Provincial headquarters within 40 days after the declaration of the result of the election in accordance with section 175(1)(a).

Section 209 of the same law provides that when filing a petition, a deposit of K2, 500.00 must be lodged as security for the cost. But it is section 210 which is the operative clause in so far as strict application is concerned. It reads:

> Proceedings shall not be heard on a petition unless the requirements of sections 208 and 209 are complied with.

In the *Ninkama* case, the respondent contended that the petition could not be heard because the witnesses attesting the signature of the petitioner had not added their occupations as required by section 208(d) of the Organic Law. The petition was ostensibly correct in all other aspects, that is, it was properly executed by the petitioner and showed substantive grounds challenging the election; yet it was struck out for failing to comply with the obligation of witnesses to supply their occupations. Although the error was minor the court said:

> It may be said the requirement that a witness' occupation must be stated is not important, or that it is not suitable to the circumstances of the country. But the method of disputing an election given by sections 206 and 208 of the Organic Law is a right given by statute. The Organic Law gives no power to hear disputes with any other requirements.

The Court went on to explain that it was not simply insisting on a rigid rule, but it was following the expressed words of the statute. The court explained that:

> ...it seems to us that the statute has clearly expressed its intention that a petition must strictly comply with section 208. It is not difficult to see why. An election petition is not an ordinary case... it is a very serious thing. It is basic and fundamental that elections are decided by the voters who have a free and fair opportunity of electing a candidate that the majority prefer. This is a sacred right and the legislature has accordingly laid down very strict provisions before there can be any challenge to the expression of the will of the majority...

Similarly on the issue of time limits the court said that they:

> ...were intended to make a definite cut off point after which there would or could be no further questions about the result of the elections. The electorate is entitled to be in no doubt as to who is its Member. The peculiar nature of this jurisdiction and the importance of the public interest of securing an early determination of the matter are relevant considerations against extensions of time and amendment of petitions...

Because the Supreme Court took such a firm position on what seemed to be a minor technical error, the courts have since held that *any* error shown in a petition is *likely* to be fatal to the petitioner. It is 'likely' because while petitions in the past two elections have been struck out for such errors, it should not have necessarily been fatal to the petition as valid grounds still remained to be tried.

The court concluded that sections 208, 209 and 210 are in mandatory terms and unless there was compliance with these provisions, there could be no proceedings on the petition as a matter of law.

The court also put into perspective section 217 of the Organic Law which provides that:

> The National Court shall be guided by the substantial merits and good conscience of each case without regard to legal forms or technicalities, or whether the evidence before it is in accordance with the law of evidence or not.

The Supreme Court said "this is the closest provision of any Organic Law which might touch on the question of dispensing with any requirements precedent,... (but) it is quite clear to us that section 217 of the Organic Law is only relevant where the National Court determines the merits of the case and when dealing with the evidence before it as relevant to the merit. It is a procedural section only". The court also rejected the argument that substantial compliance would be sufficient.

Thus, the *Ninkama* decision encapsulates the whole basis of determination of election petitions, that is, strict compliance. And while it might have been expected that such a strict approach might have softened a little since 1982, this has not really occurred.

I attribute this lack of change to two factors. These are the massive increase in election petitions and regrettably—it must be highlighted—the standard of drafting of petitions has meant many have failed to pass even the most casual scrutiny. It is disappointing for at least two reasons. Firstly, the failure to bring before the National Court properly drafted petitions that proved serious malpractices that defeated the franchise of electors. Secondly, no serious attempt was made to rectify this situation even though there was an opportunity to do so in a convention held prior to the 1997 Elections.

Grounds of Election Petitions

The actual grounds for disputing elections range from the criminal offences of bribery and undue influence to illegal practices and electoral irregularities. These are governed by section 215 which states that the election of a successful candidate will be void if he is guilty of bribery or undue influence. However, if the undue influence or bribery is committed without the knowledge and authorization of the winning candidate, the result of the election will not be vitiated. Also if the illegal practices or electoral irregularities are not likely to affect an election result, the election will not be vitiated.

It should also be noted that section 218 states that immaterial errors should not vitiate an election. The above grounds and the National Court's interpretation of these grounds constitute the grounds for review in the Supreme Court.

Increases in Election Petitions

The Papua New Guinea Law Reports (PNGLR) recorded eight petitions in respect of the 1982 elections and about 17 following the 1987 National Election. But there was a marked increase of over 60 petitions in relation to the 1992 Elections and following the 1997 Elections, there were 89 challenges for the 109 electorates. With such numbers of petitions, many of which relied on multiple grounds and required large amount of courts' time, the decisions from 1992 onwards reflected the court's insistence on compliance with section 208.

Following the increase of election petitions after the 1992 election, it was anticipated that a similar rise would occur in 1997. This prompted the formulation of new *Practice Directions* which was released by the judiciary prior to the Election in 1997.

Those *Practice Directions* were promulgated on the basis that early intervention and monitoring of cases was part of the court's obligation to provide prompt, and hopefully economic, means of resolution of the petitions. This shift in focus was targeted at parties with vested interest in delaying the outcome or attempting to defeat an opponent by a war of attrition in costs.

The new *Practice Directions* and pre-trial conferences enabled the courts and the disputing parties to narrow the issues and reduce the number of petitions by striking out those that did not comply with the *Directions*. However, the *Practice Directions* also generated multiple applications for review emanating from interlocutory decisions. The *Practice Directions* also lengthened the overall election petition process.

The National Court records show that following the 1997 Election, 89 petitions were filed.[1] Out of these 89 petitions, 25 applications for judicial review went before the Supreme Court in respect of those petitions. The increase in the number of petitions in the National and Supreme Courts impacted greatly on the judiciary. And in one case, the proceedings took more than four years to resolve that the time elapsed for a by-election if the petition was successful.

By mid 2001, there were three election reviews still pending in the Supreme Court. And on the 1 of November 2001, one of the last two cases was dismissed. One of the grounds for dismissing the review was that the relief sought (which was a by-election) was no longer available because section 106 of the *Constitution* (as amended) prohibits a by-election in the 12 months prior to a general election. Another ground for dismissing the case was that if the sitting Member was unseated because of the alleged errors of the Electoral Commission, it would be unfair to that Member and leave the electorate unrepresented in Parliament.[2]

The strict and limited process envisaged by the Organic Law and the Supreme Court in the *Ninkama* case was to ensure a one-stop shop for prompt disposal of election challenges. However, the manner in which disputing parties have readily resorted to judicial review as a means of resolving the election dispute and the amount of time allocated to resolving these disputes has shown that the current review process is inadequate and is an impediment to achieving that aim.

The Supreme Court has followed the first of those provisions that insists on the letter of the Organic Law. The other injunction of the Organic Law is that the decision of the National Court shall be final. According to section 220, there is to be no appeal from the decision of the National Court. Thus, there have been no appeals. Instead, there have been numerous judicial reviews.

The Supreme Court has ruled in a number of cases, including *Avia Aihi* [1981] PNGLR 81, *Danny Sunu & Ors* [1984] PNGLR 305 and *Kasap v Yama* [1988-89] PNGLR 197, that the Supreme Court's power of review is not restricted by section 220. The court's power emanates from section 155(2)(b) of the *Constitution*. This provision empowers the court to review all actions of the National Court by way of review *in the interest of justice where there are exceptional circumstances and cogent reasons are shown.*

Since there are no rules of the Supreme Court requiring leave to apply, parties can go directly to the Supreme Court and ask it to review an election petition. These wide provisions encouraged an influx of election petitions reaching the Supreme Court. And it is fair to say that, in many cases, the treatment of such reviews were hard to distinguish from appeals. This can be partly explained because of the broad operating principles of the *Avia Aihi* and *Kasap v Yama* and other earlier cases which confirmed that the *Constitution* vests on the Supreme Court, unrestricted power of review.

But the wide principles of *Avia Aihi* and the other cases mentioned above did not anticipate the situations where a statute, particularly an Organic Law, precludes any right of appeal. The review then must of necessity be restricted to the judicial review process which is concerned only with the decision making processes. To intervene other than that would be to grant an appeal which the Constitution prohibits. That has come to be recognized by the Supreme Court over the two decades since *Avia Aihi* and more recently in *Moi Avei v Maino*. In the latter case, the Supreme Court said that while section 220 excludes any right of appeal it does not exclude the supervisory jurisdiction of the court through the judicial review process. The point to stress here is that a judicial review is not a substitute for an appeal.

An appeal is by way of a rehearing of the trial issues where the appeal court may make its own assessment of the evidence and accept or reject the conclusions of the trial judge. In contrast, in a judicial review, only the decision-making process may be reviewed.

So in election petitions the only challenge that may be entertained by the Supreme Court is the claim that the National Court's decision was made in excess of its jurisdiction, that is, the decision was one the National Court was not entitled to make. Applications for review have rarely challenged the process of hearing an election petition. And none have sought review on the grounds that they were denied a hearing. The applications for review range across all the relevant grounds that may be relied on to overturn an election—illegal practices, electoral errors, and omissions—largely claiming that the National Court's determination was in error of law or basically not a reasonable conclusion as to the drafted petition.

There can be no challenge to the right of parties seeking relief by way of a judicial review in an election petition proceeding. But the Supreme Court, in the interests of justice, must ensure the exercise of its review jurisdiction is appropriately applied. While leave is presently not required, it is suggested that leave be incorporated into the review process by appropriate rules. It is also proposed that review should be open only at the time of the review of the substantive determination of a petition and not for any interlocutory orders as they occur.

Conclusion

There is no doubt that the readiness of disputants to resort to judicial review has stalled several petitions for months and even years, to the advantage or detriment of the petitioner or the sitting Member. There have been moves made recently by the Supreme Court to alleviate this problem, not only in matters of election disputes but also other review and appeal situations where interlocutory rulings have become predominant. The judiciary must seriously consider restricting interlocutory appeals and reviews to those going to the trial process.

Notes

* Judge of the National and Supreme Courts of Papua New Guinea.

1. Figures supplied by the Supreme Court Library.
2. *Julius Chan v Ephraim Appelis* (SCR 35 of 2000).

Chapter Five

The Role of the Judiciary in Defining and Developing the Electoral Laws

*Camillus N Narokobi**

Introduction

The purpose of this chapter is to highlight some aspects of the electoral laws that have developed so far in this jurisdiction. The experiences of conducting election petitions after the 1997 Election clearly show that the laws are still in a 'state of flush'. It is suggested that there is a need to settle the law in this jurisdiction through the development of the underlying law or even through parliamentary interventions.

In this chapter I will outline some of the areas of the electoral laws and practices which I have experienced in my role as a lawyer. Discussions will focus on the issue of interlocutory applications for stay of the decisions of the National Court and other related issues.

Election Law

The principal legislation governing election petitions is the *Organic Law on National and Local-level Government Elections* (OLNLGE).[1] It is an Organic Law made pursuant to section 126(1) of the *Constitution.* According to section 11(1) of the *Constitution*, the OLNLGE, as an Organic Law is a *Constitutional Law* and, therefore, a supreme law of Papua New Guinea. The development of this area of the law can be traced to the various decisions of the National and Supreme Courts since independence. The evolution of this body of law has been influenced largely by the decisions of the National and Supreme Courts arising from election petitions from the various National and Provincial and now the Local-level Government Elections.

National Court Sitting as Court of Disputed Returns

Section 4 of the OLNLGE provides that:

> ...any question as to whether a person has been validly elected as a Member of the Parliament or whether the seat of a Member has become vacant shall be determined by the National Court.

And section 206 of the *Organic Law* stipulates that:

> ...the validity of an election or return may be disputed by petition addressed to the National Court and not otherwise.

The wording of the provision in section 4 is in mandatory terms. This indicates that no other court has original jurisdiction to determine an election dispute except the National Court. In this jurisdiction, the National Court sits as a Court of Disputed Returns and determines all election disputes. In the past this jurisdiction was not given to the court but to a tribunal.

The power of determining other aspects of election disputes such as criminal offences relating to elections is actually shared by the District Courts and to some extent the criminal law courts. It is suggested that election petitions can be dealt with expeditiously if all questions relating to enrolment and other related matters referred to in Division 7 of Part XVIII of the Organic Law and, in particular, section 270 are dealt with by the District Courts.

In the exercise of its jurisdiction, the National Court sitting as a Court of Disputed Returns is not bound by the usual rules of procedures and evidence.[2] This also means that, it is not strictly bound by the *Evidence Act*. The court is empowered under the Organic Law to decide questions before it according to its best conscience and the principles of equity. Section 217 of the Organic Law provides that:

> The National Court shall be guided by the substantial merits and good conscience of each case and without regard to legal forms or technicalities or whether evidence before it is in accordance with evidence law or not.

This loose nature of the process appears to be a major contributing factor to the uncertainty of settling the law on both substance and form. This has led to the influx of motions and interlocutory applications. This was quite evident after the 1997 Elections. Those with the money exploited the situation to the detriment of the affected electorates and also wasted valuable court time.

It is suggested that the courts and lawyers, should apply this provision throughout the proceedings rather than waiting until the evidence is called. If this approach is adopted, the lawyers will assist the courts expedite the resolution of election petitions.

Unlimited Powers of the National Court

The National Court's power to consider an election proceeding is drawn from the *Constitution* and the Organic Law, and the Common Law as adopted by PNG prior to independence.

Armed with these powers, the courts have carved out for themselves particularly after the 1997 General Elections, a very unique status. These powers were invoked by the courts to consider all sorts of applications. As a result, the courts were confronted with many unnecessary interlocutory applications at the same time. This turn of events put enormous pressure on the judges and also created a real danger of disputing parties losing their footholds on the primary issues at stake.

The Supreme Court's power, on the other hand is limited and, if not expressed clearly, should not be invoked unless an application involves grave injustice to a party. In this circumstance, the power to review is to review a judicial act where a very clear error is manifested. This onus must be discharged by way of leave or through compulsory conferences. This would be one way of reducing issues going to the Supreme Court because the interpretative powers or enforcement powers of the court is not exercised.

Application to Strike Out

The term 'Application to Strike Out' has become synonymous with the exercise of National and Supreme Court judicial powers, especially in relation to election petitions. And yet there is no specific procedure or rule provided for in the *Practice Directions* or any National or relevant Supreme Court rules governing election petitions. The courts have, however, used the general powers pursuant to sections 155, 162, 184 and 185 of the *Constitution* to deal with this issue. The Organic Law also allows the courts to adopt their own rules of procedure. Using these provisions, the courts can and have ruled and overruled each other on various occasions on many matters of facts and law. After the 1997 Elections, we have watched with awe and disbelief judges over-ruling each other without due care to the principles of *stare decisis* of law, and the judicial duty to coherently develop the underlying law as required by the *Constitution.*

Striking out motions or applications has its parallel from the *National Court Rules* which allows for matters to be brought to the court through motions on any matters or for summary judgments. Motions of competence of petitions have often caused delays and uncertainties when the petitioners forget the nexus between the pleadings and the relief sought.

There is no doubt that some provisions must be made for interlocutory applications to *strike out'* in election petition proceedings. This tool can be appropriately used where the grounds for the petition are not properly pleaded (as required by many case laws including the principles in *Delba Biri v Bill Gimbagl Ninkama* [1982] PNGLR 342). The lack of rules of procedure in the Organic Law and the lack of other appropriate rules have resulted in a flood of applications being made at various stages of the proceedings.

The Law in a State of Flush

Since the 1997 General Election, the electoral laws have been stretched more than ever before. The courts and lawyers' efforts to do their best for their clients have generally, given little effect to finality and conclusions of court decisions in election disputes.

Section 220 of the Organic Law is unequivocally clear. It explicitly states that the decision of the National Court is final and conclusive and should not be questioned in any way. The section reads:

> A decision of the National Court is final and conclusive and without appeal, and shall not be questioned in any way.

It is suggested that the latter terms of the provision surely mean that the decision cannot be questioned in any way, even by a review. If it does not, then what did the Parliament intend when it enacted the provision? The leading case which has stretched the law to its extreme limit, is that of *Sir Julius Chan v Ephraim Apelis (No. 2)* (1999)

SC591. In that case, some more principles of law have been added by the Supreme Court, thus making it quite impossible to know if the election petition law will remain the same after the 2002 Elections.

There are three principles which became prominent in election disputes after the 1997 Election. These were: (1) the application of the 'Slip Rule'; (2) the extension of 40 days time limit accorded for filing petitions; and (3) the unlimited time period for filing a review and prosecuting the case. Lawyers should be mindful of these principles because no doubt they will emerge again after the 2002 Election. If the Supreme Court uses some ingenuity, at least some of these principles should be either overruled or clarified soon.

One of the main reasons for the uncertainty that now exists in the law is because the courts with the support of over-zealous lawyers have performed their function without any appropriate rules of procedure. The absence of any requirements for leave before a review can be entertained by the Supreme Court, may have also contributed to all sorts of applications going before the Supreme Court. It is therefore, prudent to require leave prior to any application for review.

It is obvious that we have not really been fair to the objective of the Organic Law as it applies to the people in the electorates. Unless the decisions of the courts are finalized quickly, the constituencies will remain in suspense without knowing who their elected parliamentarian is until the next election.[3] Any laws or rules relating to the prosecution of reviews should provide for specific time limits to prosecute with due diligence. If this is the case for civil and criminal appeals, then surely there should be a cut-off point for election petitions due to public policy demands.

Finality of National Court Decisions

It is clear that section 220 of the Organic Law prohibits appeals from the decisions of the National Court. The practice so far has been that parties have unashamedly capitalized on the inherent power of the Supreme Court to review actions of the National Court, through interlocutory applications, to shorten or delay the finality of election proceedings.

It is interesting to note that the courts and lawyers have not readily and sufficiently applied sections 11 and 12 of the *Constitution* to speedily bring election petitions to an end. These two provisions deal with *Constitutional* Laws which include the Organic Laws. By applying these two provisions together with sections 217 and 220 of the Organic Law, an election petition can easily be brought to an end within a reasonable time.

Section 11 of the *Constitution* declares that an Organic Law is a *Constitution Law*. There is no dispute about this. And because it is a *Constitutional Law*, it must be treated as such and be applied accordingly.

Section 11 declares that the *Constitution* and the Organic Laws is the supreme law of Papua New Guinea. This simple fact has been underestimated in many election petitions. Although the Organic Laws are supreme law by virtue of s 11, according to section 10 of the *Constitution* they are subject to the *Constitution*. This means that if there is an express interpretation in the *Constitution* giving guidance to the manner of reading or giving meaning to a term, then it should be read in favour of the *Constitutional Law*.

However, where an Organic Law's provisions are clear and unambiguous in the nature of say, section 220, then the Organic Law being the supreme law cannot be questioned at all. This argument is consist with the provisions of section 12(1)(b) of the *Constitution* which provides that:

> For the purposes of this *Constitution*, an Organic Law is a law made by the Parliament that is "not inconsistent with this *Constitution*".

Therefore, any judicial review seeking to question the finality of the National Court decisions are, *prima facie*, invalid and ineffective unless, there is a clear error. In such cases, the applicant must demonstrate to the Supreme Court by providing evidence and allowing for rebuttals or responses that there is a clear error by the National Court.

Efficient Way to Dispose off Election Petitions

There are a number of problems relating to election petition proceedings. These problems are created by petitioners, witnesses and lawyers and, to some extent, the courts. Where the problems are more peculiar to the petitioners and witnesses, it is incumbent on the lawyers to ensure that the petitions are resolved quickly.

In order for a petition to survive, it must meet the pleading test. This requirement is well understood, but often not met due to poor drafting by lawyers and even lack of sufficient instructions. It is obvious that the first cause is often the main reason. After the 1997 General Elections, many election petitions were allowed to continue despite rulings or findings by judges that the pleadings were bad, or insufficient for voiding an election result.

The pleading of allegations must set out specific particulars. This includes factors such as the actual act complained of; individuals involved; time and place of the allegation complained of; and if it is criminal in nature, then it is necessary to plead the elements of the allegations as set out in the *Criminal Code* or the *Summary Offences Act*.

Many lawyers and sometime judges have difficulty understanding or differentiating an error from an illegal act capable of voiding an election as defined in the Organic

Law or the *Criminal Code*. This lack of understanding has led to numerous difficulties encountered by the parties and unfortunately prolonged petitions. Some petitioners have also become incensed with the assumption that given this malady they could easily obtain a cotton ball from shreds of fabric. Lawyers are also equally guilty of fishing for technicalities to sustain what are otherwise bad election petitions.

For instance, if an electoral official made the error in not properly assisting an illiterate person in casting his or her vote, this error has been treated as an illegal practice capable of affecting the result of an election. Despite the fact that an error is incapable of voiding an election on its own, the petitioners often hope that they could turn it into an illegal act in the same way as bribery or undue influence. This has often caused unnecessary delay in determining the petition.

The failure by clients or petitioners in paying their legal costs can also be a major reason for delaying the resolution of a petition. The lawyers should be aware that they cannot just drop the petition for non- payment of fees because the judges will not accept this reason very lightly.

Fair Election

One of the first issues that the National Court wants to satisfy itself with is whether there was indeed an election conducted according to the law. This task will be made easier if the pleadings are drafted properly in accordance with the requirements of the Organic Law. If the court is satisfied on this issue on the face of the pleadings, the next issue it needs to consider is whether the total election in the electorate was conducted fairly. These are issues which must be addressed at the early stages of the proceedings. When disputing parties have reached an agreement on this and other related issues, the only issues left to be tried by the court will be those that are capable of voiding the election.

It is suggested that where acts or omissions of a criminal nature are identified in the election proceedings, they should be referred to the criminal courts for determination in the first instance. This is necessary given the fact that the flexible rules of evidence and procedure used in an election proceeding would not guarantee a fair trial to the winning candidate.

An important issue that has not been considered seriously and in some detail by the appropriate agencies is the disparity of numbers between the total number of eligible voters obtained before an election and the total number of votes cast in the election in a number of electorates. The total number of votes the winning candidates obtains in an electorate compared to the total number of eligible voters in an electorate has never been fully investigated by the Electoral Commission and other relevant authorities. Where there emerges a clear disparity of votes in an electorate, the election result is suspect and the matter must be investigated immediately. In the 1997 General Elections there must have been more then three electorates where this situation occurred. And yet the agencies charged with the powers to ensure a fair election failed to do anything about it.

Representation by Lawyers

The Organic Law contains a proviso regulating the appearance of lawyers before the courts in election disputes. The representation by lawyers in an election proceeding is not a matter of right. Section 222 of the Organic Law states that:

1. A party to a petition shall not, except by consent of all parties, or by leave of the National Court, be represented by counsel or solicitor.
2. In no case shall more than one counsel appear on behalf of a party.

In some of the leading cases which emerged after the 1997 General Elections, up to three lawyers were representing one party with little regard for the *Constitutional Law* requirement. The granting of leave was never even considered by the disputing parties and the courts.

An even more serious concern is the representation by overseas counsels. It is suggested that in the future the engagement of foreign counsels in election petition proceedings should be discouraged. As far back as 1979 in the case of *Jordan v Edwards* [1979] PNGLR 420, the court held that foreign assistance would not normally be required where issues involve the construction of the *Constitution.* Applying this principle to the OLNLGE, it is clear that it is an Organic Law, and as such, is a *Constitutional Law,* and therefore, the involvement of foreign lawyers in its construction should be either limited or prohibited altogether. Papua New Guinean lawyers have a better knowledge of the *Constitution* and the Organic Law and therefore, they are better placed to resolve election disputes more appropriately than their foreign colleagues. After the 1997 General Elections, some petitions did not proceed to trial because the parties were able to work out some amicable solution to end the disputes. The disputing parties in these cases were usually represented by local counsels who knew each other well and so were able to reach a solution easily and quickly. The chances of settlement with foreign counsels in similar cases are, however, less likely.

Reviews and Special Courts

Judicial reviews are distinct from appeals. In this jurisdiction, some lawyers and judges have disagreed with each other on this issue in a number of cases. And in election petition cases, it is now generally accepted that there cannot be an appeal. However, despite this agreement, election reviews are not strictly governed by the *Supreme Court Act*, although the legislation provides for reviews in general.

It is suggested that if appropriate rules are developed by the courts specifically for reviews of election petitions in the same way as the appeals in criminal and civil jurisdictions, it would result in election petitions being dealt with expeditiously.

It is also suggested that special courts be created under section 172 of the *Constitution* to deal primarily with election petitions. This point was made at the first pre-trial conference in an election petition proceeding after the 1997 Elections. It was also pointed out that judges be appointed to deal exclusively with election petitions. This idea might have to be considered seriously as part of the preparations for the 2002 Elections. If established, these courts could also deal with disputes between provincial governments and the national government because this area of the law is still evolving.

In 1997, it was observed that there were reviews upon reviews and the recalling of decision and review of decisions following the failure of parties to succeed in recalling decisions. Some parties had more than one bite at the cherry than others. And in some instances, some parties had three or more bites of the same cherry!

Trial

The trials of petitions can be hastened if there is no difficulty with the witnesses and the evidence. The discovery process has not really caused much difficulty. There is, however, no need to have too many witnesses on every single allegation. At the trial it is likely that there will be many witnesses. The large pool of witnesses should be reduced to no more than two for every issue or allegation. In *Sir Julius Chan's* case, the trial took almost two weeks to complete. And the transcript was 802 pages long. The case had a total of 10 written judgments, four Supreme Court decisions, six National Court decisions and three other related court decisions.

A total of 11 judges presided over one or another matter of the case in both the National and Supreme Courts. The lawyers who were involved in this lengthy legal battle included a legal firm from Australia and at least three law firms and a total of 11 lawyers, and a total of 86 witnesses. The petition covered a period of almost five years.

Recount

In the last National Election, a number of results in election recounts were unnecessarily subjected to undue delay. This happened where the results of the recounts were declared by the courts at different times. This situation should not happen in the future. The result of a recount should be declared by the court almost immediately in a special court sitting. In *Sir Julius Chan's* case the result of the recount was declared by the court almost three months after the completion of the recount.

Some parties have also tried to find fault with the preparations for recounts and claim substantial relief in the later stage of the proceedings. This practice should be discouraged because it casts serious doubts on the genuineness of the petitioners and can also cause undue delays.

There should, however, be different procedures for dealing with such complaints through the normal law enforcement agencies. Even at this stage (recount), reviews should not be allowed on matters arising from the procedural aspects of recounts or errors and omissions of Electoral Commission officials.

The relief of recount should be determined in the initial stages of the proceedings. It may be more efficient to determine this issue at that stage, especially if there are serious questions involved. Where recount is one of the reliefs requiring trial, then it is necessary to proceed to trial first before the court can decide whether to grant the relief or not.

In the *Sir Julius Chan* case, some of the grounds which were dismissed earlier by the court were later restored by the same court for no other reason than a recount. At the proceedings, efforts were also made to circumvent the trial by proceeding first to a recount. An interlocutory application for this purpose was made, but declined. Maybe in the future, this procedure can be used effectively to quickly put to an end an election petition. However, lawyers and petitioners must be aware that section 170 of the Organic Law allows for a recount after the counting if the difference between the winning candidate and the runner-up is less than 0.25 per cent. Perhaps where the percentage is less than 0.25 per cent that court can grant an application for recount if it had not been done following the counting.

Security for Costs

The current arrangements for security for costs is sufficient. However, it is suggested that where an election petition extends beyond say two years, the party disputing the election must be ordered to pay extra costs. Unless this is done, those with the money will end up being the only ones pursuing their rights before the courts. In the last election, it was evident that those with the money fought tooth and nail to continue their petitions even though some of the petitions were bad from the very beginning.

Findings of the Court

It is suggested that strict conditions be imposed on parties that intent to question the findings of the court following a full trial. These conditions should be incorporated into relevant procedures that may be formulated in the future. It will also help if the limitations governing appeals contained in the *Supreme Court Act* are extended to election reviews.

In the case of *Charles Maino v Moi Avei* the Supreme Court made a surprise ruling following the recount based on new evidence which disputed the manner in which the recount was conducted. The petitioner had relied on this new evidence to invalidate the election of Mr. Avei. The decision caught many people by surprise. An application was made to the same bench to reconsider its decision. The application was accepted by the court and it quickly changed its decision. It is important to note that because it is a Supreme Court decision, the National Court and the Supreme Court will have to apply it in the future. It is imperative for judges to be cautious in their findings and rulings. This point is critical because some parties have since the 1997 Elections, made blunders by mounting reviews simply on the judge's comments in a case.

Conclusion

The law on elections is in a state of flush. Election petitions proceeding from the 1997 National Elections has revealed huge gaps in the law. There is an urgent need to close these gaps in the law on elections before the 2002 National Election. The experiences have gained in the past few years since the 1997 Elections should encourage the judges and the lawyers to work together to rectify the situation. The law has to be clarified and settled in this jurisdiction quickly so that the law can promote the stability of our Parliament and strengthen the business of governing this country.

Notes

* LLB (UPNG), LLM (USA), Principal, Narakobi Lawyers.

1. No. 3 of 1997.
2. See section 217 of the Organic Law.
3. This was the situation in the Sir Julius Chan case. The people of Namatanai Open Electorate were kept in suspense as to who their true leader was until 1st November, 2001 when the Supreme Court stuck out the case. It had taken almost five years for the people of Namatanai to know that their elected leader was Ephraim Apelis (the sitting Member).

Chapter Six

Preventing the Abuse of Elections Through Judicial Innovation and Intervention

*Eric L Kwa**

Introduction

The procedure for resolving election petitions provided by the *Organic Law on National and Local-level Government Elections* 1997 (OLNLGE) is an important legal tool aimed at ensuring that politicians who get elected to the national Parliament are people of integrity and good standing in the community. The mechanism acts as a warning to candidates who stand for public office that if they engage in corrupt, illegal and irregular practices during an election they are likely to be ousted where such activities are proven against them in the court of law.

To protect the elections from these illegal practices, accessibility to the courts was encouraged through simple rules and an easy procedure for settling an election dispute. These rules and procedure have over the years been refined to a large extent so that it is no longer easy for an ordinary person to seek redress from the courts for election-related matters. This has come about because of the propensity of the aggrieved parties to engage lawyers who take over the carriage of their cases. And because lawyers are trained to be legalistic and formal, they have weaved the rules and procedure under the OLNLGE to suit their circumstances.

The complex procedural rules, the increasing legal costs and the delay in obtaining orders from the courts have all contributed to the decline in accessibility of the courts by the ordinary citizens. On the other hand, there are those who frequently visit the courts after almost every election. These are the well-to-do citizens who are able to afford the cost of the petitions and who do not really care about the delays. Their primary objective is to become parliamentarians.

This chapter deals with a specific aspect of the electoral process where the judiciary is engaged in election disputes. The chapter examines the role the courts play in determining the election of a candidate through the judicial review process and ends with some proposals for reform.

Reformation of the Electoral Laws

On the day of independence, the *Organic Law on the National Elections* (OLNE) became operational. It was one of the legislation that was enacted before independence and was a provisional law.[1] When the *Constitution* became operational, the OLNE also came into force.

The OLNE remained in operation until 1997 when it was repealed and replaced by the *Organic Law on National and Local-level Government Elections* (OLNLGE). The OLNLGE came into operation in that year and was first applied to the 1997 National Elections.

The principal difference between the OLNE and the OLNLGE is the provisions relating to the local-level government elections, which has to be conducted simultaneously with the elections for the Parliament. The insertion of these new provisions also created a different route for seeking remedies for election disputes for local-level government elections.

Election Petitions under the OLNLGE

Election petitions are initiated under Part XVIII[2] of the OLNLGE. An election petition is addressed to the Court of Disputed Returns (which for all practical purposes is the National Court) pursuant to section 206.[3] The format for an election petition is set out in section 208. This is a mandatory provision.[4] It sets out five different items that must be fully quantified by the petition. The petition must:

- contain the facts relied on to invalidate the election or return;
- specify the relief sought;
- be signed by the petitioner or person qualified to vote at the election;
- attested to by two witnesses whose full particulars must be stated; and
- be filed at the registry of the National Court within 40 days after the declaration of the election result.

An election petition lacking any one of these items or lacking clarity of any of these items can prove very fatal to the petitioner's cause. The following cases clarify this point. In *Greg Mongi v Bernard Vogae and the Electoral Commission* (1997) (EP No. 49 of 1997), the petitioner did not comply with two of the five limbs of section 208 and thus, the court dismissed the petition. A similar mistake was made by Albert Karo in *Karo v Kidu* [1997] PNGLR 28 and Norman Fernadez in *Norman W. Fernadez v Philip Taku* (1997) N1662. In *Kela v Lafanama* [1997] PNGLR 151, the petition was struck out by the court because the petitioner made the simple error of not obtaining the signatures of his witnesses on his petition.

An election petition is a serious matter and should not be treated lightly. The Supreme Court commenting on section 208 observed that:

> It seems to us that the statute has clearly expressed its intention that a petition must strictly comply with section 208. It is not difficult to see why an election petition is not an ordinary cause and it is a very serious thing.[5]

Most election petitions fail at this preliminary stage of the proceedings usually by way of preliminary objections[6] to the drafting of the petition. The rules relating to the screening of election petitions at the preliminary stage were settled in *Biri v Ninkama* [1982] PNGLR 342 and *Holloway v Ivarato* [1988] PNGLR 99. The same principles are now applicable under the OLNLGE.[7]

The OLNLGE also provides certain grounds upon which a petitioner can rely on to dispute the election of a successful candidate. These grounds are:

- undue influence [section 215(1)]
- bribery [section 215(1)]
- illegal conduct by voters [section 212(4)]
- treating [section 101 of the *Criminal Code*]
- procedural irregularities by Electoral Commission officials [section 215(3)]

An election can be declared null and void if the petitioner can prove that the successful candidate unduly influenced the voters to vote for him or her in the election. The relevant authorities on this subject are: *Nerville Bourne v Manasseh Veto* [1977] PNGLR 298, *Andrew Wabira v Payale Elo* [1977] PNGLR 328 and *Malipu Balakau v Paul Torato* (1982) MP 132 of 1982.

Where the petitioner can successfully prove that the successful candidate committed bribery, the election can be declared null and void. However, if the elements of bribery are not proven by the petitioner, the petition can fail as Albert Karo realised in *Albert Karo v Carol Kidu* (supra). Bribery committed by supporters of a winning candidate without his or her knowledge and authorization will not result in the nullification of the election. The elements of bribery established by the courts under the OLNE[8] were reaffirmed under the OLNLGE by the court in *Albert Karo v Carol Kidu* (supra) and *Komane Wasege v Mathias Karani* (1998) N1696.

Illegal conduct by supporters of a candidate can result in the invalidation of an election. If the gravity of the conduct would not affect the result of the election, this ground will fail. Thus, *in Kandep Tindiwi v The Electoral Commission and Ors* [1987] PNGLR 128 where 7,634 votes were destroyed by angry voters, the court ruled that the outcome of the election would not have been affected by the loss of the ballot papers.

Election petitions that pass the litmus test proceed to normal trial.

Judicial Review of Election Petitions

The relevant procedure for judicial review of a decision of the National Court is through an application to the Supreme Court pursuant to section 155(2)(b) of the *Constitution.* This route is permitted by the Supreme Court because section 220 of the OLNLGE bars an appeal from the decision of the National Court.

An application for judicial review is usually made to the Supreme Court. Table 1 shows the number of election petitions for the 1997 Elections that went for review before the Supreme Court. All these review applications were made in one of two stages or at both stages at different times. The first was at the end of the trial of an election petition where final orders were made. And the second was at the end of a preliminary hearing where interlocutory orders were made. In the latter, a preliminary order was accepted as the final order if the dismissal of the petition, was accepted by the petitioner. The third, but not a common situation, was applications for judicial review permitted by the Supreme Court to review its own decision.

Table 1: Summary of Applications for Judicial Review in the 1997 Elections

Case Type	*Grounds Appeal*	*Case Year*	*Registered*	*Dealt with*	*Pending*
SC Rev	Election Petition	1997	23	23	0
SC Rev	Election Petition	1998	53	53	0
SC Rev	Election Petition	1999	12	11	1
SC Rev	Election Petition	2000	5	5	0[9]
Total			**93**	**92**	**1**

A number of observations can be made about the figures set out above. First, given that there are 109 seats in the national Parliament, one would assume that almost 83 per cent of the seats were disputed in the National Court. This is not the case because some of the applications were filed by the same parties to the one and same election petition. For example, the election dispute between Sir Julius Chan and Ephraim Apelis involved three review applications; Dick Mune and Anderson Agiru involved four review applications; Daniel Kapi and Takai Kapi had five review applications; and David Basua and Charles Luta also had five review applications.

The second observation is that the number of application for review increased in 1998 because it was in that year that decisions in most election petitions were delivered by the National Court.

The third observation is that the five applications for review in 2000 did not emerge from the normal course of things (i.e. trial in the National Court). As is clearly

Table 2: Applications for Judicial Review filed in 2000

Case	*Ground Type for Review*	*Case Year*	*SCA No*	*Applicant (s)*	*Respondent(s)*	*Decision*
SC R	Election Petition	2000	9	Electoral Com	John Mesueng & Richard Koronai	29/9/00
"	"	"	13	Daniel Tulapi	Charles Luta & David Basua	10/10/00
"	"	"	24	Daniel Kapi	Kelly Aiok & Takai Kapi	28/07/00
"	"	"	35	Julius Chan	Ephraim Apelis	1/11/01
"	"	"	51	Daniel Kapi	Kelly Aiok & Electoral Commission	

indicated in the preceding paragraph, these cases proceeded from 1997 to 2000 because of a number of preliminary and subsidiary issues that had to be dealt with first before a final order could be issued from the National Court. This is shown in Table 2.

Application for Leave to Apply for Judicial Review of Election Petition

In a normal civil and criminal proceeding, leave is sought before a review is conducted by the Supreme Court. In applications for judicial review of election petitions made pursuant to section 155(2)(b) of the *Constitution*, there is no need to seek leave. The issue was settled by the Supreme Court in *Aita Ivarato v Peti Lafamana and Electoral* Commission (1998) SC 563. In this case the applicant had filed an application for leave to apply for judicial review of the election petition. The Supreme Court said that:

> ...it is not necessary to address the question of leave in detail because as we indicated to counsel, leave in relation to review of election petitions have been granted as a matter of course, because the Organic Law [OLNLGE] precludes any right of appeal.[10]

The Supreme Court made this ruling because "[I]n the present case, there is no statutory right of appeal or review, therefore, the jurisdiction for review emanates from a constitutional right and the application is based on section 155(2)(b). There is no statutory right or statutory provisions requiring leave to be granted before the Supreme Court can review decisions pertaining to election petitions".[11] In *Application of Herowa Agiwa* [1993] PNGLR 136, the Supreme Court declared that invoking its power under section 155(2)(b) is a right.

Grounds for Applications for Judicial Review

An application for judicial review in an election petition case must satisfy one or all of three principles. These principles were first enunciated in the famous case of *Avia Ahia v The Sate* [1981] PNGLR 81. In that case the Supreme Court had to decide on a question of whether the applicant had a right to invoke the power of the Supreme Court under section 155(2)(b) after her right to appeal was time-barred. The Supreme Court ruled that the applicant could seek leave to invoke this power. The power vested in the Supreme Court by section 155(2)(b) is an inherent power and can be dispensed with by the court if the applicant can prove to the court that: (1) it is in the interest of justice; or (2) there are exceptional circumstances; or (3) there are clear legal issues meriting review.

These cardinal principles of judicial review were adopted and applied in election petition cases beginning with *Balakau v Torato* [1983] PNGLR 242. The same principles have also been held to be applicable under the

OLNLGE by the Supreme Court in *Daniel Kapi v Takai Kapi and Electoral Commission* (1997) SC 548; *Aita Ivarato v Peti Lafamana and Electoral Commission* (1998) SC 563 and *Jimson Sauk v Don Polye and Electoral Commission* (1999) SC 6.

The majority of the 25 recorded cases that went before the Supreme Court had to rely heavily on the above principles to attract the attention of the Supreme Court. Some attempts were made to stop the applications from proceeding before the Supreme Court on the grounds of competency. For example, in the bitter legal battle between Peter Peipul and Pila Niningi for the Imbongu Open Electorate, Niningi tried unsuccessfully to prevent the proceeding in *Peter Peipul v Pila Niningi and Electoral Commission* (1998) SC 580 from continuing on the grounds of competency. Unfortunately, Niningi's term as the new Member for Imbongu Open was cut short by the decision of the Supreme Court in the above case.

An effective strategy frequently used by disputants to temporarily bar the review from proceeding is the demand for the payment of security for costs into court. This strategy was attempted in *David Lambu v Peter Ipatas and Ors* (1999) SC 601 and *Perry Zeipi v Gabia Gagarimabu and Electoral Commission* (1999) SC 611. Both attempts were unsuccessful. Where this strategy has been successful and the applicant for review has failed to comply with the order, it has proven fatal for the defaulting party.[12]

The lodgement of an application for judicial review does not prevent respondents from raising these and other grounds to put an end to the election petition.

Judicial Review as an Obstacle to Justice

An application for judicial review can become a nightmare for various people for different reasons. This is apparent, especially where applications for judicial review are successfully made at the preliminary stage and during the course of the trial. A case in point is *Charles Maino v Moi*

Avei and Electoral Commission (1998) N1733. This was a contempt proceeding brought against Charles Maino after he made certain comments in the media against Moi Avei. Maino was frustrated after the National Court ordered a recount of the votes for the Kairuku Hiri Open Electorate and Moi Avei immediately filed an application in the Supreme Court to review that decision of the National Court. Maino, obviously frustrated by the application for review, said words to the effect that:

> I hope lawyers are not appealing just for the sake of appealing in order to make money out of the Electoral Commission which is funded from the public purse [.] what is my brother Moi afraid of now [?] Is he afraid of the recount? Is it because he is trying to hide something?

An application for review is also costly. The case of *Julius Chan v Ephraim Apelis* (supra), *David Lambu v Peter Ipatas and Electoral Commission* (supra) are on point. It is also expensive to run an election petition in the National Court. The total cost of the 84 election petitions filed in 1997 and the five (5) filed in 1999 paid to the respondents' lawyers after taxation amounted to K796,537.76.[13] The largest amount paid to a respondent's lawyers after taxation on record is K124,116.15.

An election petition is also very time-consuming. On average an election petition conducted in the National Court takes approximately 12 months to complete. For simple applications for review it takes less than six months to resolve. Review applications involving complex and supplementary issues usually take longer to complete. It is important to highlight here that the long delays in resolving election disputes are attributed mainly to the emergence of supplementary issues raised at the preliminary hearings in the National Court and the

Supreme Court where an application for review has been filed. From the evidence available it is clear that the courts have quite successfully dealt with the majority of the election petitions expeditiously. The majority of the applications that have found their way to the Supreme Court were usually rejected or dismissed by the Supreme Court expeditiously. At present there is only one case before the Supreme Court outstanding from the 1997 National Election. That is the case of *Daniel Kapi v Kelly Aiyok and Electoral Commission* (SCR No 51 of 2000).

In these lengthy legal battles, it is the electors of the electorate who suffer most. This suffering is reflected in two main ways. First, the electorate is kept in suspense, not knowing who its truly elected leader is. The cases involving the Imbongu Open Electorate, the Namatanai Open Electorate and the Wabag Open Electorate are good examples. Second, the people from the disputed electorate cannot access goods and services provided through their elected representative due to the inability of the elected representative to perform his or her duties effectively because of the uncertainty of his or her parliamentary position.

In the final analysis, it is really the people who suffer more than the disputants of the election. While the disputants are fighting for power and control of the electorate in the courtrooms, the voters are left stranded in the electorate confused and frustrated.[14]

Proposals for Reform

Given the considerations highlighted above, there is a serious need to reform the current rules and procedure for review of election petitions by the Supreme Court. Some of the areas, which are relevant for consideration are set out below.

The measures provided by the OLNLGE for the resolution of election disputes are aimed at ensuring that elections are conducted in a free, fair and lawful manner. The role of the judiciary in the electoral process is vital to the fulfillment of these aims. The participation of the judiciary in the process is also to encourage and promote the rule of law.

In an election petition, the judiciary is being asked to determine whether the election was conducted freely, fairly and in a lawful manner. The underpinning of the process is to preserve the voters' choice.

Some of the relevant issues that require consideration are:

- Should judicial review applications be made from interlocutory/preliminary orders? Or should interlocutory applications be entertained and determined separately in the course of the trial or at the end of the trial? Or further still, should judicial review applications be made from final orders?
- Should leave be granted for all judicial review applications from interlocutory or final orders?
- If leave is required, what should be the grounds for granting leave?
- What are the standards of scrutiny? Should they be strict or flexible?

In relation to the first issue, one only needs to look at the number of review applications that have been rejected by the Supreme Court in the first instance to take a position on this matter. The majority of the review applications from interlocutory orders in the last elections that were rejected by the Supreme Court clearly signal that new rules have to be formulated to regulate this aspect of election disputes.

It is suggested that application for judicial review should only be made after the National Court has issued the final orders. Applications for review from interlocutory orders or during the course of the trial should be discouraged. To allow applications for review at this early stage when there exists an opportunity to do the same after the final orders can be described as "having two bites at the cherry". The importance and the role of preliminary hearings was observed by the court in *Michael Nali v Stephen Mendepo and Electoral Commission* (1998) SC 542:

> The court has allowed for a procedure for preliminary objections to ensure that such matters are dealt with expeditiously as possible. These preliminary objections are not designed to deliberately hinder the petitioner going to trial.

However, if interlocutory applications are permitted, then it is suggested that rules on leave applications (with appropriate modifications) be introduced for this type of proceedings. Only after the Supreme Court is satisfied that the rules have been complied with can an interlocutory application be entertained. It follows that if this proposal is adopted stringent grounds for leave must be formulated.

The Supreme Court has now settled the second issue. This position should not be altered given that section 220 of the OLNLGE bars any appeal from a decision of the National Court. However, what needs consideration is the necessity to control the propensity of applications from interlocutory orders given during the course of the trial. Applications from preliminary orders should be subjected to the rules on leave applications. The rationale being that such orders are not envisioned by section 220, and thus cannot obtain the same kind of prominence given to final orders.

The next issue then is: what grounds should be formulated to grant leave? And whether these grounds should be flexible or rigid. In view of the majority of the reviews that have been dismissed by the Supreme Court after the 1997 Elections, stringent grounds should be developed to prevent the courts from being flooded with frivolous and unmeritorious applications.

It is tempting to suggest that rules similar to those that are currently applicable in applications for leave before the Supreme Court should be adopted in election petition cases. It is imperative to distinguish between the procedure and grounds for review because of the caution raised by the Supreme Court in *Desmond Baira v Kilroy Genia and Electoral Commission* (1998) SC 579. On a question of whether the court should adopt the procedure on 'a no case submission' in an election petition case, Kapi DCJ (with whom Hinchliffe J and Jalina J fully agreed) said:

> In my opinion, it would be a mistake to readily adopt a procedure, which is applicable in criminal proceedings. The intention of the legislature is clear that proceedings under the Organic Law [OLNLGE] are different and therefore, it is fundamentally wrong to adopt procedures from other type of proceedings. I adopt the same approach I took in ... in respect of adopting procedures of consolidation in other civil proceedings. What procedure is adopted for proceedings under the Organic Law [OLNLGE] is a matter for judges in their law making power to prescribe under section 212(2) of the Organic Law... The court should be guided by the substantial merits and good conscience of each case without regard to legal forms or technicalities.

It is, therefore, suggested that the grounds relied on to seek leave in an application for judicial review in the National Court under Order 16 of the *National Court Rules* should be adopted and modified to suit election petition cases. In the event that this proposal is considered, it is suggested that grounds such as *locus standi* should be rejected because the parties have already satisfied the requirement in their appearance before the National Court, and timing should either be rejected or modified to make it as short as possible.

In determining leave the court is exercising its discretion judicially.[15] The principal ground should be whether the applicant has an arguable case. What criteria should the court adopt to determine this issue? It is suggested that it be left to the Supreme Court to develop the criteria based on a case-by-case basis.

Conclusion

The resolutions of election disputes were originally intended to be a simple matter for ordinary citizens. Over the years the rules and procedure for resolving this kind of dispute have become more complicated for the ordinary citizen. The lawyers and the disputing parties have now become the central players in this concert.

It is unlikely that we can turn the clock back to recapture the intent of the Parliament when it enacted the OLNE and later the OLNLGE. The way forward is to design rules and practices which will promote justice and fairness to the people who have exercised their right to elect their representative to the Parliament.

Notes

* Former Executive Dean of the School of Law and Business Studies, UPNG, and currently doing Ph.D in Law at the Faculty of Law, University of Auckland, New Zealand. I record my thanks to Mrs. Miriam Walo, the Acting Law Librarian Michael Somare Library (UPNG), Mr. Lohia Raka, Director, Policy and Planning, NJSS and Mr. Tom Dangiaba, the Court Librarian, National and Supreme Court Library for providing me with valuable information which has been used in this chapter.

1. Several Organic Laws were enacted prior to Independence on 16 September 1975 by the House of Assembly

(legislature) which were to become operational to avoid any vacuum in the law at Independence.

2. Sections 206-233.
3. For disputes in connection with local-level government elections, the starting provision is section 287.
4. This is the clear stipulation of section 210.
5. *Re Dibela Biri v Bill Ninkama* [1982] PNGLR 342 at p 345. The OLNLGE adopts verbatim section 208 from the OLNE. The only exception being that under the old section 208(d) the time for filing a petition was four months whereas under the new section 208(d) it is now 40 days.
6. For a clear analysis of preliminary objections see the National Court decision in *Karo v Kidu* [1997] PNGLR 28.
7. This observation was made by the court in *Karo v Kidu*, supra.
8. See for example *Kagul Koroka* v *Thomas Negints* (1982) N390 and *Richard Moaitz v Tom Awasa* (1983) N424.
9. There remains only one election petition for review before the Supreme Court. On Thursday 1 November 2001, the Supreme Court put an end to the long drawn out saga between Sir Julius Chan and Ephraim Apelis for the Namatanai Open Seat.
10. *Aita Ivarato* v *Peti Lafamana and Electoral Commission* (1998) SC 563 at p 2.
11. Ibid.
12. The long running legal battle between Chan and Apelis (*Julius Chan v Ephraim Apelis* (SCR 35 of 2000)) was finally put to an end on 1 November, 2001. One of the grounds for dismissing the case was that the applicant, Julius Chan could only manage to pay half the security for cost.
13. Figures provided by the National Court Registry through Mr. Lohia Raka, Director, Policy and Planning on 1 November, 2001.
14. This view was expressed by the Supreme Court in *Melchoir Pep v Puri Riyong and Electoral Commission* (1999) SC 614.
15. See *Geno v PNG* [1993] PNGLR 22 and *NTN P/L v Tele Corp* [1987] PNGLR 70 for a discussion on this subject.

Chapter Seven

EXPEDITING ELECTION DISPUTES IN THE COURTS

*Lawrence M Newell ISO**

Introduction

The purpose of this chapter is to deal with some of the issues that affected the Supreme Court and National Court Registries that occurred after the 1997 National and Local-level Government Elections. Due to insufficient information on local-level government election petition issues they will not be dealt with. However, the issues which are addressed in this chapter are relevant also to magistrates, district court staff, lawyers and litigants, especially on the subjects of carefully *crafted case* flow management principles and *a rigid use* of a set case assignment system by judges, magistrates, court staff, and lawyers.

Deposits

One of the major problems experienced by the Registry is identifying and disbursing the K2,500.00 paid by election petitioners as security required under the *Organic Law on National and Local-level Government Elections* 1997 (OLNLGE).

The security for election petitions (K2500.00) is paid into the 'Registrar, National Court Trust Account' (No. 5551), at any branch of the Papua New Guinea

Banking Corporation (PNGBC). An additional K50.00 for filing fee is paid to the Consolidated Revenue in the usual way. It is important that when the petition is delivered to a Court House, the deposit slip with the stamp of the PNGBC applied to it must be attached to the petition.

However, on many occasions where the deposit is made with PNGBC, the petitioners fail to produce the bank deposit slip to the Registry staff to enable them to identify which funds in the account relate to which matter. As a result, the Registrar has been unable to pay out the portion of the petitioner's or respondent's costs from the K2,500.00 deposited.

Taxation of Costs

Another issue that affects the disbursements of funds from the 'Registrar-National Court Trust Account' is that in many instances it is unclear whether the Registrar pay out all or part of the deposit.

The following extract from a letter recently written to the lawyer for the Electoral Commission illustrates the point:

> In addition please contact the Lawyer for the 1st respondent to ensure that he is not having his Bill of Costs taxed, otherwise we can only pay you Kl,250.00.

If the order is to pay the respondent's costs, the Registrar can pay only Kl,250.00 to the Electoral Commissioner as the second respondent, and if as occurs sometimes, the first respondent fails to have his or her costs taxed, the Registrar retains the other K1,250.00 until it is clear whether the first respondent will have his or her Bill of Costs taxed. At this stage the Registry does not have a solution to this issue.

Applications to Dismiss for Want of Prosecution

In the National and Supreme Court Registries there are files which have never been disposed off. These include appeals to the Supreme Court and applications to the National Court on elections and a range of other matters dating back well before independence. The Registry is also holding millions of Kina in both the Registrar's and Sheriff's Trust Accounts for actions that were never discontinued.

According to the records at the Registry the following is the status of election petitions arising from the 1997 National Election as at October 2001:

- Total number of election petitions withdrawn or discontinued—13.
- Total number of election petitions struck out or dismissed by the National Court—36.
- Total number of election petitions dismissed upon Supreme Court review—33.
- Total number of election petitions upheld—6.
- Total number of election petitions pending—1.

From the above figures, it is significant to observe that from the total number of petitions filed after the 1997 Election, only one petition remains unresolved. Before the 1997 Elections, the Registry still had some pending election petitions which were not completed from previous elections since independence. Thus, the resolution of 99 per cent of the petitions from the 1997 Election is encouraging for both the litigants and the other parties involved in election petition proceedings.

It would help the Registry if prior to the return of the writs for the 2002 Elections, the Electoral Commission could apply to the National Court by motion and dismiss all outstanding election petitions. This will enable the database of election petitions at the Registry to be tidied up.

Late Filing of Election Petitions

The OLNLGE requires that an election petition must be filed at the National Court Registry within 40 days[1] after the declaration of an election result. However, on many occasions, those lodging election petitions have complained about late filing due to the Registry being closed. This argument is flawed because the Registry can be opened at any time of the day or night on any day of the week at the amazing cost of K5.00.[2] The Registrar's telephone number is also in the Telephone Directory and he or she can be contacted on the phone for assistance.

The issue of late filing has now been settled in *Chan* v *Apelis and Electoral Commission* (SCR 71 of 1997) and so should not be of any major concern in the near future.

Caseflow Management

The National Court, conscious of the need to improve case processing time of election petitions introduced the individual docket system (IDS)[3] after the 1997 Elections. This important initiative in case management of election petitions require judges to 'manage' their own docket. The key features of IDS are:

- Increased judicial involvement and management in all stages of proceedings.
- A single judge is randomly allocated to a case from commencement to disposition.
- Individually tailored directions, procedures and listings for each case and monitoring of compliance with orders.

Close and continuing supervision by judges under the IDS allows them to deal effectively with trouble areas of litigation, such as defective pleadings, excessive discovery of documents and tactical games by lawyers.

The success of IDS in processing election petitions was, however, hampered by the frequent difficulty in getting a hearing before a busy docket judge, and the variable case management practices evolving as individual judges developed their own management styles and practices.

These difficulties are not peculiar to Papua New Guinea. As Solomon and Somerlot observed the success of any particular system:

> may be due to the accountability and judicial control built into the particular court's plan and skill and commitment of the judges rather than to any inherent system difference.[4]

The basis of effective caseflow management according to Solomon and Somerlot is built on the following principles:[5]

- Judicial Commitment and Leadership
  The system only works if all the judges and court staff are committed to making the system work.
- Court Consultation with the Bar
  Lawyers must be consulted by the judges and court staff, understand what is expected of them, and be committed to making the system work.
- Court Supervision of Case Progress
  The judges, court staff and lawyers must play an active role in determining the timetable, which will govern all proceedings during the life of a case. There must be mechanisms built into the system to ensure that matters are monitored from filing until final payment of election deposits after taxation of a Bill of Costs.
- Standards and Goals
  There are three important standards and goals for every case:

  1. Overall time standards;

2. Intermediate standards governing elapsed time between major case events; and
3. System management standards governing adjournments and disposition of matters.

- Monitoring and Information System
  Standards and goals by themselves are ineffective unless there is an effective system to monitor performance and compare it to the standards, whether it is the individual performance requirements of a particular matter or the standards that apply to all matters within the particular area.
- Scheduling for Credible Trial Dates
  A critical component of effective case flow management is that if matters are fixed for hearing of interlocutory matters or the final trial, then the matter must proceed on the day and time stated. Preparation for trial by lawyers must occur at a certain time prior to the interlocutory and final hearing dates. If lawyers know that the matter will proceed on a certain date there can be no excuse for poor preparation. However, if a particular judge or the court is known to vary dates then caseflow management ceases to work effectively.
- Court Control of Adjournments
  Solomon and Somerlot call this 'Court Control of Continuances'. Whether you speak of continuances or adjournment, the principle is the same—the court must focus on the principle that lawyers properly prepare for matters before it. And the matter proceeds on the date fixed for the number of days that all lawyers in the matter agree the matter should proceed for. Adjournments should be extremely minimal.

Conclusion

In this chapter the seven principles of caseflow management have been set out in detail because the adherence to carefully crafted caseflow management principles and a rigid use of a set case assignment system by judges, magistrates, court staff, lawyers and their clients (the litigants) in election petitions is the key element in getting petitions dealt with promptly and efficiently.

Judges, magistrates, court staff, lawyers and litigants need to work together to produce better rules and procedures (including a better database) in sufficient time prior to the 2002 National and Local-level Government Elections. This will enable the principles of the case assignment system and caseflow management to be fully understood by those involved with election petition cases when the petitions start to flow into the District Court and National Court after the 2002 Election.

Notes

* Registrar of the National Court and Supreme Court.

1. Previously, under the old Organic Law the period was four months.
2. Except that during a curfew or a national emergency the Registry officers require curfew or emergency passes to open the Registry.
3. Solomon and Somerlot call it an 'Individual Calendar System'. See Maureen Solomon and Douglas K. Somerlot, *Caseflow Management in the Trial Court* (USA: American Bar Association, 1987).
4. Id, p. 34. Their comments are based on work the done by Barry Mahoney of the National Center for State Courts in the USA in 1985—1987.
5. Id, pp 77-31.

Part Three

Selected Election and Leadership Issues

Chapter Eight

The Electoral Process and Leadership

*Ila Geno OBE QPM**

Introduction

Election time in Papua New Guinea (PNG) every five years is an exciting time. It is also a daunting time for the Electoral Commission, the candidates and the voters. After an election, it is the voters who have to live with the decision they make for the next five years. The voters determine who the country's leaders are—who will be the country's managers.

The National Election is a time when candidates promise voters and entice them in the hope of winning a seat in the Haus Tambaran (the Parliament) at Waigani. It is also a time when the Electoral Commission is busy orchestrating the election process.

The topography of the country is quite rough. In many parts of the country there are no access roads or airstrips. Therefore, the task of the Electoral Commission as well as the candidates, is sometimes difficult. They have to walk for miles, through thick tropical jungle, rugged mountainous terrain and swamps filled with mosquitoes. Some areas of the country are even dangerous to be in during the election period because of the political in-fighting between rival candidates and parties.

The Constitution

The *Constitution* gives the citizens of PNG the special right to vote and stand for public office. This right is a predominant character of a free and democratic society. This right enables the citizens of the country to determine the country's leadership.

The *Constitution* allows for an Organic Law to set out the conduct of parliamentary elections in PNG. This is also provided for in the *Constitution.* This Organic Law is the *Organic Law on National and Local-level Government Elections* (OLNLGE).

Part VI, Division 2H of the *Constitution* also provides for the protection of elections from outside or hidden influences and strengthening of political parties. Section 127 of the *Constitution* stipulates that one of the purposes of Subdivision H is:

> ... to protect elections and to prevent candidates from being, or appearing to be or to have been, improperly influenced by outside (especially foreign) or hidden influences...

Sections 129 and 130 of the *Constitution* (which are located in Part VI, Division 2H of the *Constitution*) provide for an Organic Law to guide the integrity of political parties and candidates. This Organic Law referred to as the *Organic Law on the Integrity of Political Parties and Candidates* (OLIPPC) was enacted last year. The Organic Law will come into full operation in the 2002 National Elections.

Section 127 of the *Constitution* also prohibits a "candidate or former candidate for election to the Parliament from accepting from a non-citizen assistance (financial or other) in respect of his candidature in excess of an amount prescribed by"[1] the OLIPPC.

The Relevant Laws

In this part of the chapter a brief mention of the relevant laws that regulate the election of leaders and their responsibilities will be made.

Organic Law on National and Local-level Government Elections (OLNLGE)

The conduct of parliamentary elections in PNG is provided for by the OLNLGE, made pursuant to section 126(1) of the *Constitution*. It is to be noted that section 126(3) explicitly requires that elections must be in accordance with section 50 of the *Constitution*.

The OLNLGE gives effect to sections 125, 126 and 187C of the *Constitution* by providing for:

- a Boundaries Commission;
- the defining of boundaries of National electorates;
- an Electoral Commission;
- the holding of National Elections; and
- the holding of local-level Government Elections.

The primary function of the Electoral Commission as stated by section 15 of the OLNLGE is to conduct all elections for the Parliament and the legislative arm of the local-level governments.

Organic Law on the Integrity of Political Parties and Candidates (OLIPPC)

While the *Constitution* gives every citizen the right to stand for elective public office, that right "may be regulated by a law that is reasonably justifiable for the purpose in a democratic society that has a proper regard for the rights and dignity of mankind".[2] It would appear that the OLIPPC regulates this special right to stand for elections.

This Organic Law, which the Ombudsman Commission is also required to enforce, provides also for the receiving of campaign contributions from citizens. Moreover, it provides for the duty of the candidates to declare such contributions.

Under the OLIPPC if a candidate is a member of a registered political party, the candidate is also entitled to funding of his or her election campaign by his or her political party. The political party receives election campaign funds from the Central Fund established by the Organic Law. Donations from citizens for election purposes can also be made direct to the Central Fund or to a registered political party.

The Leadership Code

Many candidates who are elected to Parliament are not aware that there is a *Leadership Code* that governs their conduct. An important matter which candidates must be mindful of is the enormity of the responsibility they are vested with once they get into Parliament.

Parliamentarians must be careful to note that as soon as they get elected, their personal interests are overridden by the interest of the country and their constituencies. Intending candidates must be aware that once they enter Parliament, they will no longer have a private life because theirs is a public life, 24 hours a day, seven days a week and 365 days a year.

It is also the responsibility of candidate to ensure that elections in which they participate in are trouble-free. They should not try to incite trouble between their supporters and those of opposing candidates.

The Electoral Commission

In conducting an election, the preservation of the integrity of the Electoral Commission's independent constitutional function to conduct a fair and open election is fundamental to our democratic system of government. Briefly the functions of the Electoral Commission are to:

- assess and update the electoral rolls;
- accept or otherwise nominations of candidates standing for elections;
- organize polling places and polling officials;
- organize and conduct elections for electorates; and
- organize and conduct all elections for the Parliament and legislative arms of the local-level governments.

As mentioned earlier, given the fact that the country is rugged, the Electoral Commission has indeed a difficult task in conducting National Elections. Some harsh criticisms have been labelled against the Electoral Commission on its handling of National Elections. However, people must appreciate the fact that conducting elections in this country is quite an enormous task.

In the last Election, over 2000 candidates contested for the 109 seats in Parliament. Ensuring that these candidates conducted a fair campaign was difficult, given the large number of candidates. The preparation of voting papers alone takes a great effort. Polling officials also have to be recruited. There are to at least, four officials who have to be appointed for each booth and there are quite a number of booths in each electorate. The Common Rolls for each electorate have to be updated. Plans have to be made and there has to be wide public awareness to inform the public on how to vote and where to vote.

The Electoral Commissioner must also appoint a Returning Officer[3] for each electorate who is charged with the duty of giving effect to the OLNLGE in his or her electorate. These officers are directly answerable to the Electoral Commissioner.

Election officers who are engaged to conduct elections must not participate in any activities which may call into question the constitutional independence and integrity of the Electoral Commission. In a case where the election's scrutiny and counting process is flawed with systemic and substantial irregularities perpetuated by electoral officials, then the result of the election cannot be said to be fair, open and democratic and therefore, valid. In such cases it is open to the court to decide whether the errors and omissions "did affect the result of the election" within the meaning of section 218(1) of the OLNLGE.

It has been alleged that Returning Officers are handpicked by Provincial Administrators and not the Electoral Commissioner. There is concern within the Electoral Commission itself that the neutrality of some of the Returning Officers is suspect. Who is in charge of ensuring that these Returning Officers supervise provincial counting in a fair and transparent manner?

It is imperative for all intending candidates for next year's elections to read the OLIPPC carefully. Because, in that law, candidates will find what is expected of them, their rights and obligations during and after the elections. An election is analogous to an athletic competition. Only one person out of the competitors will win. Most athletes know this rule and only dispute the outcome if they know they have a valid reason.

Scrutineers must be appointed by candidates to represent them at polling places during the polling. Not more than one scrutineer, other than relieving scrutineers must be allowed for each candidate at each polling booth on any one day. The appointment of scrutineers must be made by notice in writing in the appropriate form to the Returning Officer or Presiding Officer. The appointment forms must be signed by the candidates to enable scrutineers to access a polling booth. A candidate may also appoint a scrutineer to represent him or her at the counting session.

Candidates must not in any way take part in the conduct of polling and under no circumstances, must be allowed into the polling booth at any time except to cast their vote.

These are examples of some of the election activities that the Electoral Commission and candidates have to properly deal with to ensure a successful election.

Political Corruption and Vote Buying

The problem of buying elected leaders in the lead-up to the formation of governments in PNG will hopefully become less of an occurrence with the enactment of the OLIPPC. Previously, 'horse-trading' was rampant causing a lot of inconveniences to the parliamentary system and the public, but with the enactment of the OLIPPC the country should see less of this problem.

Another related problem is that of vote buying at the elections. This problem is caused mainly by the absence of a strong political party framework and the absence of laws regulating political parties and candidates. For example, in some electorates, vote buying means forcing women to vote for a candidate against their will by their menfolk. Inadequate policing at polling booths give rise to individual voters exercising their constitutional right to vote under coercion. There is no guarantee that polling teams and ballot boxes, and papers are completely safe and secure.

Preamble to the Constitution and the National Goals and Directive Principles

As the Chief Ombudsman, it is my duty to also point out the ideals our Constitution requires of all of us at the outset. It is important to point out that the Ombudsman Commission and the courts have a very specific interest in these matters, not only in enforcing the laws, but also the moral and ethical standards of our society.

The Preamble to our *Constitution* and the National Goals and Directive Principles contained in the law must be observed. Our founding fathers and mothers had tremendous vision and foresight in drawing up the Preamble and the National Goals and Directive Principles 26 years ago. These statements contain the true intent of the people of PNG which is to do greater good for the country.

The Preamble contains a number of important principles adopted at independence by virtue of the authority of the people of Papua New Guinea. These are:

- *All power belongs to the people, acting through their duly elected representatives.*
  It is important that our politicians and intending candidates take careful note of this declaration by the people through the *Constitution*. It is important to highlight that there is a duty of trust vested on *all* public offices: the officeholder is the trustee and the people of PNG are the beneficiaries. Each candidate must embrace this goal and acknowledge that all power belongs to the people in the event that he or she is voted into Parliament.
- *Respect for the dignity of the individual and community interdependence are basic principles of our society.*
  This principle is fundamental to what we as individuals and a society must respect and uphold. This declaration entrenches the principle of democracy.
- *We guard with our lives our national identity, integrity and self-respect.*
  This principle implores us to be proud of being Papua New Guineans. It also promotes the spirit of unity and implores us to maintain and promote integrity and respect for each other.
- *We reject violence and seek consensus as a means of solving our common problems.*
  This principle beckons us to resolve our problems by consensus and through non-violent means.
- *Our national wealth, won by honest, hard work is to be equitably shared by all.*

Equality and equity in sharing our wealth without discrimination is promoted by this principle.

The Preamble also declares the five National Goals and the Directive Principles of PNG. Every Papua New Guinean, including our politicians and candidates, must be guided by them. The National Goals are:

- **Goal No. 1: Integral Human Development**
  Every person is to be dynamically involved in the process of freeing himself or herself from every form of domination or oppression so that each child, man or woman will have the opportunity to develop as a whole person in relationship with others.
- **Goal No. 2: Equality and participation**
  All citizens are to have an equal opportunity to participate in, and benefit from, the development of our country.
- **Goal No. 3: National sovereignty and self-reliance**
  Papua New Guinea is to be politically and economically independent, and our economy basically self-reliant.
- **Goal No. 4: Natural resources and environment**
  Papua New Guinea's natural resources and environment are to be conserved and used for the collective benefit of us all and to be replenished for the benefit of future generations.
- **Goal No. 5: Papua New Guinean ways**
  Our development is to be achieved primarily through the use of Papua New Guinean forms of social, political and economic organization.

The *Constitution* states that although the Preamble and the National Goals are not laws that can be enforced (except by the Ombudsman Commission), it is the duty of everyone in positions of power and influence to give effect to the visions and the goals.[4] It is important that all sitting

Members of Parliament and intending candidates must take into account these principles during the coming elections as they are ideals that represent the cornerstone of our country—a united PNG.

Conclusion

The Electoral Commission is indeed working around the clock to make next year's election fair and open to entrench the notion of democratic and free elections. But for those of us who can contribute to make it a success, it is also in the interest of democracy and that of the people of PNG that we combine our efforts to make it as peaceful as possible and to ensure that good leaders are elected.

The Parliament represents the highest form of democracy and all of us have a duty to make it more useful and relevant. That is why the Ombudsman Commission has been vigilant in the performance of its functions in recent years to try and get the Parliament as an institution and its individual members to be responsible and accountable to the people of PNG.

Every Papua New Guinean has a moral and constitutional responsibility to uphold the principles adopted by the Preamble to our *Constitution* and the National Goals and Directive Principles as these are the visions and ideals that united this country and continue to hold us together. This is our modern culture.

Notes

* Chief Ombudsman of Papua New Guinea.

1. Section 130(1)(b).
2. Section 50(2).
3. The appointment of the Returning Officers must be published in the *National Gazette*.
4. Section 25(1).

Chapter Nine

Responsibilities of Candidates and Political Parties

*Ano Pala**

Introduction

In 2001, the national Parliament enacted the *Organic Law on the Integrity of Political Parties and Candidates* (OLIPPC) to regulate the activities of political parties and members of political parties. The administration of the Organic Law is vested in the Central Fund Board (Board) established by the Organic Law. In this chapter, the role, powers and functions of the Board and the composition and activities of political parties and politicians will be discussed.

The Central Fund Board

The Board is established by section 40 of the OLIPPG. There are six positions which are created by section 41 of the Organic Law. The Board comprises members who represent different sectors of the community and those institutions which play an important role in the electoral process. The membership of the Board comprises the:

- the Clerk of the Parliament, *ex officio;*
- the Electoral Commissioner, *ex officio;*
- the Chairman of the National Fiscal and Economic Commission, *ex officio;*
- the Registrar of Political Parties, *ex officio;*

- a National Council of Women representative; and
- a National Council of Churches representative.

The Central Fund Board is independent and not subject to any direction and control by any person or authority.[1] The Board is required under section 52 to report to the Parliament through the Head of State by 31 of March in each year.

The functions of the Board are set out in section 49 of the Organic Law. The Board is responsible for: (1) the consideration of applications for registration of political parties, and (2) formulating policy concerning, and for the control and management of the Central Fund. The Board has the power under section 49 (2) to: (1) raise monies, from within or outside Papua New Guinea, and (2) invest funds in bonds and securities within the country for the purposes of the Central Fund.

Registration of Political Parties

An application for the registration of a political party may be lodged at any time before, after or even during the 2002 National Elections.[2] In the case of existing political parties which were in existence before the Organic Law came into force, they are deemed to be registered, provided they lodged their application to register within six months from the day the law came into force.[3]

All political parties which intend to contest the next National Election, must be registered under the law. If a political party is not registered it will be prohibited from: (1) nominating candidates for election; (2) having members representing it in Parliament; and (3) receive public funding from the Central Fund.[4] For the purpose of the next election (2002) it will, therefore, be necessary for all political parties intending to contest the elections to register before the close of nominations.

The Board has not set a time limit by which parties must lodge their applications. However, in order to meet all the mandatory procedural requirements, an application would have to be lodged, at the latest, three months before the close of nominations for the next elections.[5]

Membership of Political Parties

Political parties are prohibited from restricting their membership on the basis of sex, race, religion or place of origin.[6] The membership of political parties are restricted only to citizens. No person can be a member of more than one political party at the same time. A person is not eligible to be a member of a political party if he or she has not paid in full the relevant membership fees required under the constitution of the party.

If a Member of Parliament who has not paid his membership fees to his or her political party, he or she will continue to remain a member of the political party for the duration of his or her term of Parliament. The political party can, however, expel a Member of Parliament from the party according to the rules provided in the party's constitution.[7]

Executive Officers of Political Parties

Section 4 of the OLIPPC provides that a political party is required to have the following executive officers of a party:

- President;
- Secretary;
- Treasurer;
- A Parliamentary Leader where the party has two (2) or more members who are Members of Parliament.

The executive officers of the political party are prohibited from holding any other public office, or being an employee or member of the governing body of a public body including a superannuation fund or a corporation in which the State has an equity interest. These positions are created by the Organic Law and because it is assumed that their terms and conditions of employment would be attractive to draw suitable applicants.

In the event that a political party does not have sufficient funds to meet the expenses relating to the employment of its party executives, it may be necessary for the State to meet these expenses. The rationale is that by making these positions attractive, the best people can be employed to these posts, and in the long term, the State would effectively strengthen the very foundation of the political party system envisage by the Organic Law.

Resignation and Expulsion from Political Party by Members of Parliament

A Member of Parliament may resign from a political party in accordance with the procedures provided by section 71 of the OLIPPC. A Parliamentarian may resign from his or her political party:

- before a general election or a by-election and within the periods allowed for resignations under the Organic Law;
- if the political party or an executive officer of a political party has committed a serious breach of the constitution of the party; or
- if the political party has been adjudged insolvent under applicable laws.

These grounds for resignation are referred to as permissible grounds under the Organic Law. In any investigation under the OLIPPC or the *Organic Law on the Duties and Responsibilities of Leadership*, the Member who has resigned has to prove that the grounds for his or her resignation were permissible grounds under section 70(2) of the OLIPPC.

Where a Parliamentarian resigns from a political party, the president of the party is to immediately inform the Registrar of Political Parties about the cessation of membership of the Parliamentarian to the party. The Registrar is then required to refer the Parliamentarian to the Ombudsman Commission for investigation. The Ombudsman Commission, following investigations in accordance with its procedures shall make a decision as to whether or not the Member of Parliament has committed an offence which amounts to a misconduct in office.

If the Ombudsman Commission decides that the Parliamentarian is not guilty of a misconduct in office, the Member of Parliament may remain as an independent Member of Parliament or join another political party. If the Ombudsman Commission is satisfied that the member is guilty of a misconduct in office, the matter shall proceed in accordance with Part V of the *Organic Law on Duties and Responsibilities of Leadership*.

A Member of Parliament may be expelled from a political party in accordance with the constitution of that party. The expelled Member may remain an independent Member or join another registered political party of his or her own choice.[8]

Funding of Political Parties

A political party can only be funded in accordance with the Organic Law. According to section 53 the funds shall consist of:

- funding from the Central Fund;
- contribution from citizens and non-citizens; and
- any other income not inconsistent with the Organic Law.

From the Central Fund, a political party will receive K10,000.00 per annum for each of its members who are

Member of Parliament.[9] A citizen or a non-citizen can contribute up to a total of K500,000.00 in respect of political parties in any calendar year and up to a total of K500,000.00 for a candidate in respect of any one election.[10]

A person (a citizen or non-citizen) who makes a contribution to a political party or a candidate must, within 30 days of making that contribution, inform the Registrar of the amount of the contribution, and the name of the political party or the candidate to whom the contribution was made, and the date it was made. A registered political party or a successful candidate is also required to inform the Registrar within 30 days of receiving the contribution, the details of that contribution.

Entitlement to Funding from the Central Fund

A Member of Parliament who is not a member of a registered political party is not entitled to receive any funding from the Central Fund. A registered political party will also not receive funding from the Central Fund if it does not have a Member in Parliament.[11] Moreover, a registered political party which has Members in Parliament, but has failed to file a financial return in accordance with the Organic Law will not be entitled to any funding from the Central Fund.[12]

Funding of Female Candidates

Women have been given special recognition and encouragement to stand for elective public office by the OLIPPC. If a woman candidate sponsored by a political party loses the election, but obtains at least 10 per cent of the votes cast in the electorate in that election, the political party will receive 75 per cent refund of the expenses it incurred in endorsing the woman candidate.[13]

Two conditions must however, be proven, by the political party to obtain the refund. Firstly, the political party must be registered in accordance with the Organic Law. And secondly, the Board must be satisfied that the registered political party is entitled to funding under the law.

Financial Returns by Political Parties and Candidates

A registered political party is required to lodge with the Registrar of Political Parties its financial returns within three months after an election. Thereafter, the political party is required to lodge an annual financial statement with the Registrar containing details of: (1) all contributions received by the party, (2) other receipts and incomes; and (3) all expenditures incurred during a year.[14]

A successful candidate must lodge a financial return with the Registrar, within 3 months after an election. The financial return must specify the contributions he or she received and the details of the expenditures incurred by him or her in connection with the election.[15] A successful candidate who does not file a financial return is guilty of misconduct in office.

Rights of Voting on the Floor of Parliament

There are four specific parliamentary activities which involve the casting of votes which are regulated by the OLIPPC. These four situations are spelt out in section 77. Under this provision, a Member of Parliament can only vote in accordance with a resolution of his or her party in relation to a:

- motion of no confidence in the Prime Minister;
- vote for the election of a Prime Minister under section 145 of the Constitution;
- vote for the approval of the national budget; and
- vote on a constitutional law.

The Member of Parliament may, however, abstain from voting in the matters listed above. A Parliamentarian who votes against the resolution of his or her party in the above matters will be deemed to have resigned from the party[16] and his vote shall not be counted.[17]

A Member of Parliament who votes against the resolution of his or her party in the cases referred to above and whose resignation has been determined by the Ombudsman Commission to amount to a misconduct in office shall refund to the political party all campaign expenses incurred by the party in supporting him or her at the elections. And section 80 of the Organic Law bars him or her from being appointed as a Prime Minister, Minister, Vice-Minister, Chairman or Deputy Chairman of a Committee of the Parliament for the remainder of his or her term.

Independent Members of Parliament

An independent Member of Parliament may join a political party after the election of a Prime Minister after the general election. An independent Member of Parliament who voted for the Prime Minister after the general election cannot vote for a motion of no confidence in the Prime Minister or a Minister headed or appointed by that Prime Minister.

However, an independent Member who joins a political party at least six months before the motion of no confidence in the Prime Minister is moved, can vote in accordance with the resolution of his or her political party.[18] In the case of a vacancy in the office of the Prime Minister the independent Member may vote for any candidate in the election of the next Prime Minister.

A Member of Parliament who stood as an independent candidate and who remains as an independent Parliamentarian, is not permitted to vote on two important issues. These are: (1) a vote for a motion of no confidence in the Prime Minister, or the Ministry headed by that Prime Minister, or a Minister appointed on the advice of that Prime Minister; and (2) a vote in the election of the Prime Minister following the resignation of that Prime Minister if that person is again nominated to stand for election as the Prime Minister.[19]

But the law does not stop the Member who was elected to Parliament as an independent candidate from voting in the first vote for the Prime Minister following a national election. On the other hand, an independent candidate who joins a political party six months prior to the motion of no confidence against a Prime Minister is entitled to vote, but only in accordance with his or her party resolution.

Invitation to Form the Government

Following a general election, the party with the largest number of elected candidates will be invited by the Governor General, on the advice of the Electoral Commissioner, to form the government. If, however, two or more political parties have equal numbers of elected candidates, then the Governor General, on the advice of the Electoral Commissioner, will invite each of these parties to form government.[20] The election of the Prime Minister must be by a simple majority vote.

If the party invited to form the government nominates a candidate to be elected as Prime Minister, but the candidate fails to obtain a simple majority vote, the Parliament must then proceed to elect a Prime Minister in accordance with the *Standing Orders* of Parliament. The Speaker will call for nominations and the candidate with the *largest number*[21] of votes will be declared the Prime Minister.

Conclusion

The intention of the law is very clear. It is intended to create a paradigm shift so that the performance of political parties is lifted to a higher level with a view to providing political stability and promoting accountability, and transparency at the highest political level.

The *Associations Incorporation Act* has been sparingly exploited by political parties, candidates and Parliamentarians to function very loosely and poorly. PNG has a political process which has permeated corruption, instability and weak government. The challenge for PNG now is to adjust its political culture so that the purpose of the Organic Law can be achieved.

Notes

* Clerk of the National Parliament.
1. Section 49(3) OLIPPG.
2. Section 6.
3. Section 6(3).
4. Section 6(2).
5. The "next election" in this chapter refers to the 2002 National Election.
6. Section 3.
7. The expulsion of the Parliamentarian from the party does not affect his or her membership to Parliament [section 3(7)].
8. Section 75.
9. Section 56.
10. See sections 57-59.
11. Section 61.
12. Section 67.
13. Section 62.
14. Section 67.
15. Section 68.
16. Section 78.
17. Section 79.

18. Section 82(2).
19. Section 82(1).
20. Section 76.
21. **Editors' note**: The Organic Law refers to the phrase "largest number" of elected candidates. However, it is suggested that the correct phrase should have been "highest number" of elected candidates. The former relates to the electoral process using the Proportional or Preferential voting system while the latter relates to the First Past the Post voting system.

Chapter Ten

The Constitutional Aspects of Organic Law on the Integrity of Political Parties and Candidates

*Greg Sheppard**

Introduction

In the recent Supreme Court case of *Anderson Agiru v The State,*[1] the court made a very significant decision which has very wide ramifications. The case was initiated by Mr. Agiru after his powers as the Governor of Southern Highlands Province and the provincial government was withdrawn by the national government pursuant to section 51 of the *Organic Law on Provincial Governments and Local-level Governments* (OLPGLLG). Mr. Agiru had argued that the withdrawal of powers by the government under section 51 was unconstitutional because the section was not authorized by section 12[2] of the *Constitution.* The Supreme Court accepted this argument and ruled that section 51 was unconstitutional. The effect of this decision is that the provisions in an Organic Law must be *expressly* authorized by the *Constitution.* The failure to do so will render such provisions of the Organic Law unconstitutional and invalid.

In this chapter the implications of the *Agiru* case on the *Organic Law on the Integrity of Political Parties and Candidates* (OLIPPC) which was enacted recently by

Parliament will be analysed. Also some preliminary issues pertaining to section 18 of the *Constitution* which were also dealt with by the Supreme Court in the *Agiru* case will be discussed because of their significance on the concept of *locus standi* (standing) as required under sections 18 and 19 of the *Constitution*.

Preliminary Matters

Invoking the Power of the Supreme Court under section 18(1) of the Constitution.

The *Constitution* clearly enumerates under section 19 a special class of persons who can approach (locus standi) the Supreme Court to invoke its power to interpret the provisions of the *Constitution*. The list excludes provincial governors. In approaching the Supreme Court, Mr. Agiru took the route provided by section 18(1) of the *Constitution*. The Supreme Court had to first consider whether the route taken by Mr. Agiru to invoke its power was the correct procedure. In addressing this issue, the Chief Justice said:

> The application comes before this Court by a *Constitution* section 18(1) reference. In my opinion that is the appropriate process. The Referrer is not a section 19 authority. All the parties agreed that this is the appropriate process as there are no issues of primary facts that require the National Court's determination. In my opinion it is appropriate for any interested person to apply directly under section 18(1) to this Court for its opinion on the interpretation or application of any provision of a constitutional law. Any person who has sufficient interest and who does not qualify under *Constitution* section 19 should be able to come to the Supreme Court directly under section 18(1).

There is precedent for this position. In *S.C.R. No. 4 of 1980; Re Petition of M.T. Somare* [1981] PNGLR 265, the then Chief Justice Kidu said:

> Subject to the application of section 23, section 42(5), section, 57 and section. 58 of the *Constitution*, the Supreme Court has "original jurisdiction, to the exclusion of other courts, as to any question relating to the interpretation or application of any provision of a *Constitutional Law*" (*Constitution* section 18(1)). The question then is whether the Rt. Hon Michael Thomas Somare, C.H., M.P., has the necessary legal standing to invoke the jurisdiction of this Court under section 18(1) of the *Constitution*.

> I agree with and adopt these comments as being entirely applicable to this application. Anderson Agiru is the Provincial Member for the Southern Highlands Province in the National Parliament and thus Governor and Head of the Provincial Government which has been affected by the decision of the NEC in its invocation of Division 8 of the Organic Law, the subject of this application. He does not qualify as a person who can bring a reference under section 19 of the *Constitution*. The issues raised are not matters the National Court has any jurisdiction to determine. The only primary fact necessary for the reference, being the decision by the NEC, is not in dispute and therefore, it is appropriate that the reference be brought directly to this court.[3]

Kapi DCJ also agreed in the following terms:

> This matter has come before us by way of a "purported reference" under section 18(1) of the *Constitution*. The Hon. Anderson Agiru, Governor of Southern Highlands Provincial Government is designated as the

referrer. At the beginning of the hearing, I raised a preliminary issue about the precise nature of the proceeding before the Court. However, it became apparent that lawyers for Agiru, in addition to the "purported reference", filed an application in the nature of an originating process on 19th October, 2000 in the Supreme Court seeking procedural directions and declaratory orders that include:

(i) An order that Division 8 of the *Organic Law on Provincial Governments and Local Level Governments* is unconstitutional and invalid.
(ii) An order that the purported withdrawal of the powers and functions of the Southern Highlands Provincial Government by the NEC is invalid and unconstitutional.
(iii) An order that the Southern Highlands Provincial Government has full powers and functions.
(iv) An order that the appointment of Pila Niningi as Administrator of the Southern Highlands Provincial Government is unconstitutional and invalid.
(v) An order prohibiting Mr Niningi from exercising or purporting to exercise any powers or functions of the office of the Administrator, or any other office in relation to the Southern Highlands Provincial Government.
(vi) An order prohibiting the State from purporting to withdraw the powers and functions and finances of the Southern Highlands Provincial Government.

I regard this matter as an application for declaratory orders that fall within the original jurisdiction of the Supreme Court under section 18(1) of the *Constitution*. The Supreme Court has previously dealt with similar applications by way of originating process. See *Kaseng v Namaliu* [1995] PNGLR 481 and *The Hon. John Momis & The Bougainville Provincial Government In Suspension v The National Executive Council & The Right Hon. Bill Skate, The Prime Minister* (1999), SC626.[4]

It is therefore, settled law that given proper standing, the determination of constitutional issues may be brought before the Supreme Court in its original jurisdiction under section 18(1) using this procedure.

Interlocutory Applications in Constitutional Cases

An order of the nature of interlocutory injunctions, and other orders in the nature of prerogative writs are unprecedented in this jurisdiction. Although the Supreme Court has occasionally declared a legislation to be unconstitutional and invalid, it has for example never in the interim, stayed, enjoined, injuncted or suspended the operation of a legislation passed by Parliament pending the final hearing and determination of such adjudication. It is however, suggested that, the Supreme Court not only has sufficient power under the *Constitution* to make such orders, but it is also under a duty to do so.[5]

The basis of the power of the Supreme Court to make interlocutory orders to suspend the operation of certain legislation and the manner in which this power can be exercised is discussed below.

Where the jurisdiction of the Supreme Court under section 18 of the *Constitution* is properly examined, one finds that the Supreme Court has an "inherent power... to make such orders as are necessary to do justice in the circumstances of a particular case".[6] It is suggested that this provision makes it absolutely clear that in appropriate circumstances the Supreme Court may grant interim orders. Section 155(4) of the *Constitution* contains the real source of the court's power to make orders in the nature of interlocutory injunctions and stay orders in respect of civil matters. It is suggested that there is nothing in the *Constitution* or elsewhere for that matter which would limit the application of this provision to exclude the power to make interim orders.

The true nature of the power under section 155(4) is such that it enables the Supreme Court to "tailor its remedies to the circumstances of an individual case to ensure that the primary rights of a party are protected".[7] This clearly supports the argument that the Supreme Court has the power to make orders in the nature of interlocutory injunctions and other interlocutory orders in the nature of prerogative writs.

Section 158(2) of the *Constitution* is also relevant in that it requires the Supreme Court to give paramount consideration to the dispensation of justice in interpreting the law. If interlocutory orders are required in constitutional references for the proper dispensation of justice, there can be no doubt that such a power can be found within the ambit of section 155(4).

It is also suggested that section 57(3) of the *Constitution* expressly creates the basis upon which the Supreme Court may make orders granting interlocutory relief. Section 57 of the *Constitution* provides for the protection and enforcement of rights or freedoms *"referred to in this Division"*. Section 57(3) expressly authorizes the Supreme Court to make all such orders and declarations as are necessary or appropriate for the purposes of section 57, and in particular that it may make any order... in relation to a statute at any time after it has been made (whether or not it is in force). This provision would allow the Supreme Court, for example, to prohibit the coming into force of a statute in the limited context that the statute on its face abrogates constitutionally guaranteed rights and freedoms.

It is further argued that in the absence of any express provision enabling the making of interlocutory order, the Supreme Court may turn to section 22 of the *Constitution* for guidance. The section reads:

> The provisions of this *Constitution* that recognize rights of individuals (including corporations and associations) as well as those that confer powers or impose duties on public authorities, shall not be left without effect because of the lack of supporting machinery or procedural laws, but the lack shall, as far as practicable, be supplied by the National Court in the light of the National Goals and Directive Principles, and by way of analogy from other laws, general principles of justice and generally-accepted doctrine.

In the case of *In re Moresby North East Election Petition* [1977] PNGLR 429 it was suggested that if certain provisions of the *Organic Law on National Elections* were invalid, then the National Court did have the power and indeed a duty under section 22 of the *Constitution* to provide the necessary procedures to ensure that a citizen's right to stand for election to Parliament is not defeated by an ineligible candidate.

If the suspension of the operation of this Organic Law had been requested, to ensure that a citizen might stand for election to Parliament and not have the right to be elected defeated by an ineligible candidate, it would certainly have been granted. The court also noted that in exercising its functions, it could apply those statutory provisions as appropriate to safeguard and enforce those rights.

Where there is a lack of procedural machinery to make interlocutory orders, section 22 empowers the Supreme Court to supply such procedural machinery "by way of analogy from other laws, general principles of justice and generally accepted doctrine". Interlocutory injunctions and stay orders are such principles and doctrines by the analogy referred to in section 22 of the *Constitution*.[8]

Is the Parliament or the Constitution Supreme?

This issue has become controversial lately given the decision of the Supreme Court in *SCR No. 3 of 1999: Re Sitting of Parliament*.[9] This case was initiated by the Ombudsman Commission before the Supreme Court after the Parliament decided to take a long adjournment (seven months) in 1999. Essentially, the Ombudsman Commission was concerned that the long adjournment by Parliament was in breach of the *Constitution*. The Supreme Court by an unanimous majority ruled that the long adjournment by Parliament was violating the *Constitution*. Many Members of Parliament refused to accept the decision of the Supreme Court and complained that the ruling by the Supreme Court was an interference in the operations of the legislature. Some Members of Parliament even incorrectly argued that the Parliament was supreme. In practical terms there may be some reluctance on the part of the courts to grant interim orders because it may be seen as an interference with the legislative process. However, one must not lose sight of section 11 of the *Constitution* which provides that the Supreme Laws of PNG are:

(a) the *Constitution*, and
(b) the Organic Laws,
and that "all acts (whether legislative, executive or judicial) that are inconsistent with them are to the extent of the inconsistency invalid and ineffective".

Clearly, the Parliament is not supreme. The *Constitution* is supreme. The *Constitution* empowers the Parliament to only make laws that comply with the *Constitution*.[10] If the legislative power is exercised contrary to the *Constitution*, the Supreme Court is duty bound to the full extent of its powers to enjoin such a breach.

The *Constitution* also obliges every person in PNG "to respect and to act in the spirit of this *Constitution*". This includes Members of Parliament. They are required to ensure that the laws they make are constitutional. The Members of Parliament are also required when taking office, to swear that they will uphold the *Constitution*.[11] It would make a mockery of the *Constitution*, if Members of Parliament were able to pass unconstitutional laws, for the purpose of taking short-term (but perhaps decisive) political advantage of such laws as long as they remain in force while the slow process of justice takes its course.

This is precisely what occurred in the case of Anderson Agiru. His term in office was unconstitutionally truncated by nearly 12 months, and the resources of the province were depleted or encumbered to such an extent as to affect the proper functioning of his public office. The *Constitution* is not to be mocked in this way by the Members of Parliament. Members of Parliament should not be able to gain *any* advantage by passing unconstitutional laws, and then relying on crucial delays to press home the advantage. The Supreme Court does not have feet of clay when it comes to protecting and safeguarding the special rights of citizens under the *Constitution*, and seeing that Members of Parliament honour their obligations as elected representatives of the people. The Supreme Court unquestionably has the power to declare unconstitutional laws invalid.

It is suggested that, in appropriate circumstances where it is necessary to protect and safeguard the rights of citizens, the court has the power, on a preliminary basis, to stay, suspend or otherwise render temporarily inoperative laws that it considers *prima facie* to be unconstitutional. In advancing this proposition, it is not suggested that it is sufficient for a party impugning the legislation to simply make an allegation that his or her constitutional rights are affected by the legislation and expect to obtain such an order. However, great and irreparable harm by the infringement of constitutional rights may be done in the time it takes for the judicial process to resolve the issue. He or she must clearly demonstrate by evidence that there is a *prima facie* case that his or her constitutional rights have been affected. Having discharged that burden, it is settled law that the onus of showing that the legislation is constitutional then falls on the party relying on its validity.[12] In the light of the constitutional provisions outlined above, there is no doubt that the Supreme Court is at liberty to make interlocutory orders to prevent such harm, including temporarily suspending the operation of a law which is *prima facie* unconstitutional.

If a legislation is shown on a *prima facie* basis, to be unconstitutional and affected citizens are suffering irreparable harm, there is no reason why the Supreme Court cannot intervene to protect constitutional rights pending the hearing and determination of the issue. The contrary proposition requires the Supreme Court to stand idly by while Members of Parliament take advantage of a *prima facie* breach of the *Constitution*. The Supreme Court is not impotent when it comes to protecting, safeguarding and enforcing the *Constitution*, even when it is on an interlocutory basis.

The Constitutional Interpretation of the OLIPPC

Subdivision VI.2.H of the *Constitution* empowers the Parliament to make an Organic Law for the "protection of elections from outside or hidden influences". The Parliament has now enacted that law called the *Organic Law on the Integrity of Political Parties and Candidates* (OLIPPC). Is the Organic Law properly authorized by the *Constitution*? Both the unamended and the amended section 127 of the *Constitution* (under subdivision H) provides as follows:

"... and an Organic Law may make provision, *in addition to the provisions expressly referred to in this Subdivision,* for achieving that purpose."

The following questions in respect of the constitutionality or otherwise of the Organic Law are pertinent:

- Are all the provisions of the Organic Law 'expressly authorized' by the *Constitution*?
- Is an Organic Law under subdivision H uniquely permitted to enact provisions that are *not* expressly referred to in that subdivision?
- Are any of the provisions of the Organic Law inconsistent with subdivision H of the *Constitution*?
- Is the Organic Law susceptible to be struck down as unconstitutional or for other reasons?

These questions involve an interpretation of constitutional provisions. In the *Agiru* case, the Chief Justice explained the correct approach to constitutional interpretation. He said:

> The approach to the task of understanding the proper meaning to be ascribed or imputed to the provisions of this home-grown *Constitution* has been amply articulated previously, and that is to discern the spirit, the purposes and the rationale that inspired the different structures of this *Constitution* in giving meaning to the relevant provisions under review. In my opinion this methodology would best accord with the intent of the *Constitution* section 158(2) that "in interpreting the law the courts shall give paramount consideration to the dispensation of justice".
> In my opinion it is in approaching the issue from this perspective, with a more purposive and liberal approach to the task of interpretation, that enables

the court to discern the legislature's intention when it effected the Constitutional Amendment and the Organic Law simultaneously. What were the purposes that inspired and motivated the legislative amendment? For that purpose it is relevant to consider the relevant constitutional provisions as they then existed prior to the amendment and what the amendments were. I do not consider that it is sufficient to engage in a purely literal analysis and interpretation of the provisions of this constitution.

This brings us to the consideration of the constitutionality of the OLIPPC. The first step is to understand what constitutes an Organic Law under the *Constitution*. An Organic Law is defined under section 12 of the *Constitution*. It states:

1. For the purposes of this *Constitution*, an Organic Law is a law made by the Parliament that is:
   (a) For or in respect of a matter provision for which by way of an Organic Law is expressly authorized by this *Constitution*; and
   (b) not inconsistent with this *Constitution*; and
   (c) expressed to be an Organic Law.
2. An Organic Law may be altered only by another Organic Law, or by an alteration to this *Constitution*.
3. Nothing in this section prevents an Organic Law from:
   (a) Making any provision that might be made by an Act of the Parliament; or
   (b) Requiring any provision to be made by an Act of the Parliament that might otherwise be so made, but any such provision may be altered by the same majority that is required for any other Act of the Parliament.

An important explanation of the nature and purpose of Organic Laws is contained in the judgment of Kapi DCJ:

Before Independence, there was no source of law known as Organic Law. At Independence, the *Constitution* created Organic Laws as a source of law (section 9(b) of the *Constitution*). It is a superior law (section 11) but subject only to the *Constitution* (section 10(a)). This special source of law was created because there was a concern for creating the *Constitution* into a very long document that would be overburdened with detail (see *SCR No. 2 of 1982* [1982] PNGLR 214 at 222 per Kearney DCJ). The constitutional framers intended to deal with major matters in the *Constitution* and leave details in these matters to be further enacted in an Organic Law within the scope authorized by the *Constitution*.

Section 12 of the *Constitution* is not descriptive. All Organic Laws must fall within the framework of this provision to be constitutional. The question that arises is: Does the Organic Law fall within the framework of section 12 of the *Constitution*? In particular, does the Organic Law make provisions for any matter that is not expressly authorized to be so made by the *Constitution*?

Failure to Properly Certify Constitutional Amendment No. 22[13] (OLIPPC)

The authorizing provisions for the OLIPPC are found in subdivision H of the *Constitution*. These provisions were however, substantially amended in December 2000. It is therefore, pertinent within the context of this discussion to consider whether those amendments were themselves constitutional.

Section 13 of the *Constitution* makes provision for the manner and form of making laws to alter the *Constitution*. Section 14(4) requires that the Speaker's Certificate given under section 110 of the *Constitution* must include the certification of matters specified in section 14(1), (2) and

(3). The copy of the relevant amendment reveals that there was sufficient compliance of section 14.

Section 16 of the *Constitution* stipulates that a failure to comply with the constitutional formalities applicable to constitutional amendments will be fatal to the amendment. The *Constitution* further directs that a constitutional amendment must be certified by the Speaker under section 110, or in his absence by the Deputy Speaker under section 108(2).

In the case of *Constitutional Amendment No.* 22, the law was in fact certified by someone entitled "Acting Speaker of the National Parliament". However, there is no such office provided for under the *Constitution* or elsewhere. It follows then that on the face of it, *Constitutional Amendment No.* 22 is unconstitutional because it was certified by a person who is not authorized to do so by the *Constitution*. It also appears from the document that the proper manner of certification as to making laws under section 110 may not have been complied with in that the Speaker (acting or deputy, as the case may be) has not certified the legislation *under the National Seal* as he or she is mandatorily required to do.

What is the National Seal? Section 3 of the *Constitution* specifies that an Act of Parliament may make provision for and in respect of the National Seal. The relevant legislation is the *National Seal Act.*[14] In the case of *Constitutional Amendment No.* 22, the law was not endorsed under the Speaker's hand as required by section 3 of the Act. It is therefore, strongly arguable that *Constitutional Amendment No.* 22 is not validly in force.

Breach of section 50 of the Constitution

It is suggested that *Constitutional Amendment No.* 22 purports to authorize the direct restriction of the right and opportunity of citizens to hold public office and to exercise the functions of those offices. For example, the office of 'Parliamentary Leader of a Registered Political Party' is restricted from holding the public office of 'Speaker' and 'Deputy Speaker' and Members of Parliament are in certain circumstances prohibited from exercising their public function of voting on certain important issues.

It is clear that *Constitutional Amendment No. 22* seeks to authorize the prohibition of a special right under section 50(2) of the *Constitution*. There are many other instances of restrictions on the right to hold and exercise the functions of public offices. Accordingly, under the provisions of section 38(2) of the *Constitution*, the constitutional amendment required an expression that it *"is made for the purpose of giving effect to the public interest"* in the matters set out in section 38(1) and a specification of the rights restricted by it. These words are mandatory. Without them, the entire law is likely to be ruled unconstitutional.[15] This point was stressed by Barnett J in *State v NTN Pty Limited* in the following terms:

> For very good reasons section 38 of the *Constitution* provides that a law that is intended to regulate or restrict a constitutional right must very carefully follow certain prescribed formalities. These are designed to bring to the attention of Members of the National Parliament that the Bill before them is intended to regulate or restrict one of the freedoms guaranteed by the *Constitution* and the reason why it is desirable to do so. The formalities are also designed to alert the public and special interest groups about what is being attempted and why. Not only is it expressly provided that the Bill must specify what freedom is being restricted but, on a fair and liberal meaning of the section, it must also clearly be specified which of the allowable listed purposes it is sought to achieve by this restrictive law.

> Unless the purpose for the regulation or restriction is also clearly stated...citizens whose rights have been affected will not be in a position to assess whether the law complies with the *Constitution* or not; they could be uncertain whether to outlay the expense to challenge the law if the State could be quietly sitting on the knowledge that the true but unstated purpose was (for instance) defence or public order.
> From the importance with which the *Constitution* treats the whole question of guaranteed rights, and adopting a fair and liberal interpretation of section 38(2), it is required that a law which regulates or restricts the exercise of a right or freedom referred to in the *Constitution's* Subdivision III.3.C—Qualified Rights, must clearly state which of the purposes specified in section 38(l)(a) it seeks to achieve. The ...Act failed to do this and for that single but sufficient reason it is *ultra vires* the *Constitution*. The whole Act is therefore, invalid and of no effect.

The contrary view (i.e., that section 38 does not apply to legislation that regulates the constitutional rights under section 50) is the ratio of the decision in *SCR 2 of 1982* [1982] PNGLR 214 at 227. However, it appears that section 50 is a right that may not be restricted under any circumstances. It is difficult to see how this argument can be overcome in so far as it applies to the Organic Law.

Conclusion

If this argument is correct, subdivision H of the *Constitution* remains as it was enacted in 1975 prior to *Constitutional Amendment No. 22*. As is evident, from the table set out in Schedule 1 and 2 to this chapter, most of the provisions of the Organic Law do not find express authorization in the unamended subdivision. Following *Agiru's* case, the Organic Law would most likely be found to be in large part unconstitutional. The contrary position could not be reasonably argued given the perceived need for the amendment in the first place.

On the other hand, if *Constitutional Amendment No. 22* is valid then the next issue to consider is whether the provisions of the Organic Law find express authority in the amended subdivision H. Assuming that they do, it is to be noted that in section 4(2) of the Organic Law there is a prohibition on the right of citizens who are officials of registered political parties to hold any other public office.

This provision and indeed others such as sections 8 and 9 prohibit the rights and opportunities of citizens to hold public office and to exercise public functions under section 50(l)(e) of the *Constitution*. Under section 38(2)(b), the right under section 50(l)(e) must be specified as one being restricted. This did not happen for Constitutional Amendment No. 22. For this and the reasons outlined above, it is suggested that the Organic Law is likely to be struck down in its entirety as being unconstitutional.

Notes

** Senior Partner – Maladinas Lawyers, Port Moresby

1. SCR No.4 of 2000. The decision was handed down on 8 October 2001.
2. This provision provides for the creation of Organic Laws which are to be enacted by Parliament setting out in detail specific matters which are described briefly in the *Constitution*.
3. Note 1 at pp 8-10.
4. Id, at pp 19-20.
5. Incidentally, prior to 1688 the Crown in England retained a prerogative to suspend the operation or execution of laws passed by Parliament. However, this prerogative was abrogated by the *Bill of Rights* (1688) (1 Will. & Mar. sess2c2). This prerogative is similar in concept to the right of the President of the United States to veto legislation passed by the Congress in that country.

6. See section 155(4) of the *Constitution.*
7. See *Aundak Kupil* v *The State* (1983) N435.
8. Section 5 of the *Supreme Court Act* also expressly authorizes the Supreme Court in the widest of terms to make orders of this nature.
9. SCR No 3 of 1999.
10. See s 109 of the *Constitution.*
11. See *SCR No. 4 of 1980* [1981] PNGLR 265 per Kidu CJ at p273.
12. *The State v NTN Pty Limited* [1992] PNGLR 1.
13. This Amendment provided for the enactment of the OLIPPC.
14. Chapter 14 of the Revised Laws of PNG
15. See *The State* v *NTN Pty Limited* [1992] PNGLR 1

Schedule 1

Section	Provision of the Organic Law	Authorizing Constitutional Provision	Restricting or Regulating Provisions according to section 50 and section 55 of Constitution
Part 1, sections 1 and 2	Preliminary—compliance with constitutional requirements and interpretation	Not Applicable	
Part 2, sections 3-7	Membership of political parties, executive officers, public officer requirement of political party to register qualifications for registration	Not authorized	

Part 3, Division 1 sections 8-15	Registrar disqualifications from office special conditions of employment resignation retirement vacation of office seal functions and duties of the registrar		
Part 3, Division 2, sections 16-27	The Register—Register and inspection and inspection and certificates, etc. and register etc. to be evidence and publication of list of political parties before National Election	Section 129	Regulating
Part 3, Division 3, sections 21-272	Registration Procedure—Application for registration of a political party and Application to be advertised and grounds for objection and referral of application to Board and Consideration of application and registration and notification of decision of Board	Section 129	Regulating

Part 3, Division 4, section 28	Amendment of Register—Amendment of Register	Section 129	Regulating
Part 3	Cancellation of Registration—Grounds for cancellation of registration	Partially section 129 otherwise unauthorised	Regulating
Division 5, sections 29-33	Notification of intention to cancel registration and Board to consider cancellation etc. and Effect of cancellation on Registration and Assets and liabilities, etc. of political party whose registration is cancelled		
Part 3, Division 6, sections 34-36	Procedures relating to an executive officer of, or a member of parliament who is a member of, a political party whose registration is cancelled—Procedures relating to an executive officer of, or a member of the parliament who is a member of, a political party whose registration is cancelled and further	Unauthorised	

	procedure and status of member after notification to Ombudsman Commission	
Part 3, Division 7, sections 37-38	Dissolution of registered political party—dissolution of registered political party and effect of dissolution of political party	Unauthorised
Part 3, Division 8, section 39	Amalgamation of registered political parties—Amalgamation of registered political parties	Unauthorised
Part 4, sections 40-52	Central Fund Board of Management—Central Fund Board of Management and Constitution of the Board and Chairman and Declaration of Office and leave of absence of member and vacation of office of member and vacancy not to affect powers or functions and meeting of the	Unauthorised

	Board and indemnity of member of the Board and functions and powers of the Board and Secretariat and Application of Public Finances (Management) Act and Reports by the Board	
Part 5, Division 1, sections 53-59	Funding political parties—Central Fund and Contribution—funding of political party only in accordance with this law and establishment of Central Fund and source of funds in Central Fund and Public funding, contributions from citizens and contributions from international organisations and contributions from non-citizens	Unauthorised
Part 5, Division 2, section 60	Endorsement of candidates	Unauthorised
Part 5, Division 3, sections 61-65	Distribution of funds from Central Fund, distribution of funds from the	Unauthorised

	Central Fund and funding of female candidates; claims for payment and membership of a member of the parliament in a registered political party and entitlement to funding from the Central Fund		
Part 5, Division 4, section 66	Offences relating to contributions and funding	Section 130	Regulating
Part 6, sections 67-69	Financial returns financial returns by political party and financial returns by candidate and false and defective returns	Section 129 and section 130	Regulating
Part 7, Division 1, sections 70-74	Strengthening of political parties, resignation from political party, grounds for and effect of resignation from a registered political party and procedures following resignation from a registered political party and further procedure and status of member during investigation, etc.	Unauthorised	

Part 7, Division 2, section 75	Expulsion from a registered political l party	Unauthorised
Part 7, Division 3, section 76	Invitation to form government	Unauthorised
Part 7, Division 4, sections 77-85	Defection from political party and voting restriction, defection from or voting against a registered political party and vote contrary to provisions of section 77(1) (c) not to be counted, and deemed resignation from office and other penalties for contravention of Section 77. Member elected without endorsement and voting in case of a motion of no confidence or in the election of a Prime Minister following resignation where the Member resigning is nominated for election and voting in the election of a Prime Minister following resignation of a Prime Minister	Unauthorised

	and in the event of other vacancies in the office of Prime Minister and voting on the national budget and voting on a constitutional law.		
Part 8, sections, 86-90	Miscellaneous—Misrepresentation by candidate and confidentiality and constitutional regulations.	Not applicable	

Schedule 2

Section	Provision of the Organic Law	Authorising Constitutional Provision	Restricting or Regulating Provisions according to section 50 and section of Constitution
Part 1, sections 1 and 2	Preliminary–compliance with constitutional requirements and Interpretation	Not Applicable,	
Part 2, sections 3-7	Membership of political parties, executive officers public officer, requirement of political party to register qualifications for registration		

Part 3, Division 1, sections 8-15	Disqualifications from office, special conditions of employment, resignation retirement vacation of office, seal functions and duties of the registrar		
Part 3, Division 2, sections 16 - 20	The Register—Register and inspection and inspection Certificates, etc. to be evidence and publication of list of political parties before National Election	Section 129	Regulating
Part 3, Division 3, sections 2l-27	Registration Procedure–Application for registration of a political party to be advertised and Grounds for objection and referral of application to Board; consideration of application, registration and notification of decision of Board	Section 129	Restricting section 25(3) otherwise regulating
Part 3, Division 4, section 28	Amendment of Register–Amendment of Register and	Section 129	Regulating

	cancellation of registration—grounds for cancellation of registration and	Partially section 129, otherwise unauthorized	Regulating
Part 3, Division 5, sections 29-33	Notification of intention to cancel registration and Board to consider cancellation, etc. assets and Effect of liabilities, etc, of cancellation on assets and liabilities, etc., of registration and political party whose registration is cancelled		
Part 3 Division 6 sections 34-36	Procedures relating to an executive officer of, or a member of Parliament who is a member of, a political party whose registration is cancelled, procedures relating to an executive officer of, or a member of the parliament who is a member of, a political party whose registration is cancelled and further procedure and status of member after notification to	Section 130 A, Partially autherized	Regulating

	Ombudsman Commission	
Part 3, Division 7, sections 37-38	Dissolution of Registered Poltiical Party– Dissolution of registered political party and effect of dissolution of political party	Unauthorised
Part 3, Division 8, section 39	Amalgamation of registered political parties— Amalgamation of registered political parties	Unauthorised
Part 4, sections 40-52	Central Fund Board of Management— Central Fund Board of Management and Constitution of the Board and Chairman and Declaration of Office and leave of absence of member and vacation of office of member and vacancy not to affect powers or functions and meeting of the Board and indemnity of member of the Board and functions and powers of the Board and	Unauthorised

	Secretariat and Application of Public Finances (Management) Act and Reports by the Board	
Part 5, Division 1, sections 53-59	Funding political parties—Central Fund and Contribution—funding of political party only in accordance with this law and establishment of Central Fund and source of funds in Central Fund and Public funding and contributions from citizens and contributions from international organisations and contributions from non-citizens	Unauthorised
Part 5 Division 2, section 60	Endorsement of candidates	Unauthorised
Part 5, Division 3, sections 61-65	Distribution of funds from Central Fund Distribution of funds from the Central Fund and funding of female candidates; claims for payment and membership	Unauthorised

	of a member of the parliament in a registered political party and entitlement to funding from the Central Fund		
Part 5, Division 4, section 66	Offences relating to contributions and funding.	Section 130	Regulating
Part 6 sections 67-69	Financial Returns–financial returns by political party, financial returns by candidate and false and defective returns	Section l29 and section 130	Regulating
Part7, Division 1 sections 70-74	Strengthening of political parties–resignation from a registered political party, grounds for and effect of resignation from a registered political party and procedures following resignation from a registered political party and further procedure and status of member during investigation, etc.	Unauthorised	
Part 7, Division 2, section 75	Expulsion from a registered political party	Unauthorised	

Part 7, Division 3, section 76	Invitation to form government	Unauthorised
Part 7, Division 4, sections 77-85	Defection from political party and voting restriction—defection from or voting against a registered political party and vote contrary to provisions of section 77(1) (c) not to be counted and deemed resignation from office and other penalties for contravention of section 77. Member elected without endorsement and voting in case of a motion of no confidence or in the election of a Prime Minister following resignation where the member resigning is nominated for election and Voting in the election of a Prime Minister following resignation of a Prime Minister and in the event of other vacancies in the office of Prime	Unauthorised

	Minister and voting on the national budget and voting on a constitutional law	
Part 8, sections 86-90	Miscellaneous–Misrepresentation by candidate and confidentiality and constitutional regulations	Not applicable

Part Four

National and Supreme Court Election Petition Rules

NATIONAL COURT ELECTION PETITION RULES

and

SUPREME COURT ELECTION PETITION REVIEW RULES

Prepared by Working Committee:

Justice Timothy Hinchliffe—Chairman, Justice Mark Sevua, Justice Salamo Injia, Dr John Nongorr, Mr Camilus Narokobi, Mr Alfred Manase, Ms Emily Dirua

Part One

National Court Election Petition Rules

for

Conduct of Election Petitions 2002

The above named rules was prepared by the Chairman of the Working Committee, Justice Timothy Hinchliffe following discussions at the Workshop held at the Gateway Hotel and discussions held by the Working Committee at its meeting held on 22/3/02, 27/04/02 and 18/05/02.

The rules was further presented and discussed at the recent Judicial Conference on Election Petitions on Friday 31st May 2002, Ballroom, Holiday Inn.

The Working Committee further deliberated on the rules on Saturday 15th June 2002. The current draft is the collaborate effort of the Working Committee to date.

The Committee would welcome further comments and suggestions to simplify the rules further whilst maintaining the need to observe the substantial requirements for natural justice and, furthermore, to expeditiously deal with those election petition matters.

General:	These rules are concerned with the procedures relating to the presentation and conduct of election petitions and may be cited as the Election Petition Rules 2002
Commencement:	These Election Petition Rules shall come into effect on 1st January 2002.

1. Place of Filing

All election petitions shall be filed in the Registry of the National Court at Port Moresby or at the Court House in any Provincial Headquarters (see Schedule 1).

2. Date of filing

The reckoning of the time limit for filing election petitions pursuant to Section 208 (e) of the *Organic Law on National and Local-Level Government Elections* shall include all days of the week.

3. Fees

The filing fee for an election petition shall be K250.00

4. Deposit as Security for Costs

The security deposit of K2500.00 required by Section 209 of the *Organic Law on National and Local-Level Government Elections* must be paid in cash or by bank cheque.

5. Service of Petition on Respondents

1. Within 14 days of the date of filing an election petition, the petitioner must serve a copy of the petition on the respondents and must at the same time provide the respondents with
   (a) three copies of a Notice of Intention to Appear completed within the title of the proceedings.
   (b) The Judge's notice stating the date, time and place at which a Direction Hearing will be held.

(2) The date referred to in 5 (1) (b) shall be within 40 days from the filing of the petition.

(3) *Respondents* in these Rules mean
   (i) the successful candidate in the election;
   (ii) the Electoral Commission;
   (iii) the Electoral Commission made a party pursuant to Section 211 of the *Organic Law on National and Local-Level Government Elections;*
   (iv) or any other unsuccessful candidate

6. Mode of Service

1. Any service under this Rule may be given by:

   (a) personal service; or
   (b) in the case of the successful candidate by leaving it with an adult person at the respondent's residential address as stated by the respondent in the nomination form for candidates prescribed by Section 85 of the *Organic Law on National and Local-level Government Elections;* or
   (c) such other service as the Court may, on application, approve.

2. Where any service is made in the manner prescribed in subsection (b) above, notice of that service shall be given to the respondent by registered mail addressed to the respondent through the Parliament House.
3. The Registrar shall send a copy of each election petition to the Clerk of the Parliament.

7. Proof of Service

A petitioner shall, within 14 days of service of the petition, file an affidavit of service at the National Court Registry at Port Moresby or at the Provincial Court House where the petition was filed indicating the manner of service and, if service was by personal service, how the respondent was identified and served, and the date of service of the petition and other required or associated documents.

8. Intention to Appear

Within 14 days after the date of service of the petition, a respondent who intends to appear on the hearing of the petition shall file a notice to that effect in the National Court Registry or the Court House in the provincial headquarters where the petition was filed and serve a copy on the petitioner.

9. Place of Trial

1. An election petition may be heard at any Provincial Centre determined by the Court.
2. In the case of the Central Province, the place of trial will be at Waigani.
3. All election petitions (and interlocutory applications) will be dealt with in the Provincial Centre where the petitions are filed unless an application is made to the Court for change of venue.

10. Production of Documents

1. All relevant documents required for the hearing of an election petition shall be filed and served on the direction of the judge at the Direction Hearing.
2. The Production of documents is the responsibility of the parties to a petition. The Court may, however, upon request by the parties, direct production of any document, record or thing that in its opinion may be necessary for hearing of a petition.
3. Where an election petition or notice is required to be published by the Registrar, the cost of the publication shall be paid in the first instance by the petitioner or, as the case may be, by the person by whom the notice was given, without prejudice to the manner in which such cost shall ultimately be borne by one or more of the parties to the petition.
4. Any summons, notice or document required to be served on any person for purpose of causing the appearance of that person before the Court, or of giving the person the opportunity of making a statement, or showing cause, or having the person heard by the Court for any purpose relating to election petitions, may be done in any of the following ways:
   (a) personal service; or
   (b) such other manner as the Court may direct.

11. Amendment of Petition

An election petition may be amended at anytime before the expiry of the time limit provided in Section 208(e) of the *Organic Law on National and Local-level Government Elections*.

12. Direction Hearings

1. At the Direction Hearing the Judge shall consider amongst other things, the following:
   - (a) whether pursuant to Section 222 of the *Organic Law on National and Local-Level Government Election* parties shall be represented by Counsel;
   - (b) the implication of the issues;
   - (c) filing of affidavits by the parties;
   - (d) the necessity to direct any electoral records to be produced;
   - (e) determining the number of trial days required to accommodate all parties;
   - (f) the date for the hearing;
   - (g) the necessity to adjourn a hearing to a Provincial Court House in or close to where the electorate is situated; and such other matters as may aid in the prompt disposition of the petition.

13. Hearing

At the hearing the Court shall deal with the petition and any challenges to the competency of the election petition and any other preliminary matters.

14. Consolidation of Petition

Where two or more election petitions relating to the same election or return are presented, they shall be heard together and as one petition.

Schedule 1

List of Cour Houses at Provincial Headquarters

#	Court House	Province (Provincial Administration name in brackets)
1.	Buka	Bougainville (North Solomon's);
2.	Port Moresby (Waigani)	Central
3.	Kundiawa	Chimbu (Simbu)
4.	Goroka	Eastern Highlands
5.	Kokopo	East New Britain
6.	Wewak	East Sepik
7.	Wabag	Enga
8.	Kerema	Gulf
9.	Madang	Madang
10.	Lorenga	Manus
11.	Alotau	Milne Bay
12.	Lae	Morobe
13.	Kavieng	New Ireland
14.	Popondetta	Northern (Oro)
15.	Mendi	Southern Highlands
16.	Daru	Western (Fly River)
17.	Mount Hagen	Western Highlands
18.	Kimbe	West New Britain
19.	Vanimo	West Sepik (Sandaun)
20.	Port Moresby (Waigani)	National Capital District

Note: For Port Moresby all petitions are filed at the main Waigani Registry with the Deputy Registrar—National Court. In all other places petitions are filed with the Clerk of Court, except in Goroka, Kokopo, Lae, Madang, Mount Hagen and Wabag where they are filed with the Assistant Registrar.

In the National Court of Justice at	MP .... of 2002

Petitioner
and
Respondent

Notice of Date and Venue of Direction Hearings

To the:

Petitioner:	
Respondent:	
Electoral Commissioner:	

I, ________________________ , in my capacity as a Judge of the National Court of Justice appoint the following date and venue for the holding of the pre-trial conference in the above matter:

Date:	............................/......................... 2002
Venue:	Court House,..................................
Dated:	............................/......................... 2002

Signed:	
	Judge National Court of Justice

Model of Letter of Advice of Service Under S.6(2) of the Election Petition Rules

Date:

'A Member'
c/- National Parliament House
P O Parliament House
WAIGANI
National Capital District
Papua New Guinea

Sir/Madam,

The purpose of this letter is to advise you that an election petition disputing your election as Member of Parliament for (*Electorate*) filed in the National Court at (*Waigani*) under number MP (1) of 2002 was served on you by leaving it with (at *your village*) the address stated in the form used by you to nominate as a candidate for the *(Electorate)*.

A copy of the petition may be obtained from the National Court Registry at Waigani. Please note that a Compulsory Conference for all parties to this petition is set down for (*9:30 a.m. 11 August, 2002*) at the National Court, Waigani.

Yours faithfully

Petitioner

cc: The Registrar
Supreme and National Courts of Justice
P. O. Box 7018, BOROKO
National Capital District
Papua New Guinea

Part Two

Supreme Cour Election Petition Review Rules For Conduct of Election Petitions 2002

Supreme Court Election Petition Review Rules

1. The Committee considered that the first issue to address is whether or not there should be any reviews allowed at all under section 155(2)(b) of the *Constitution* in view of section 220 of the *Organic Law on National and Local-Level Government Elections* (hereinafter abbreviated "OLNLGE").

   OLNLGE, section 220 provides:

   A decision of the National Court is final and conclusive and without appeal, and shall not be questioned in any way.

   Constitution, section 155(2)(b) provides:

   The Supreme Court has an inherent power to review all judicial acts of the National Court.

   Constitution, section 155(4) which is relevant provides:

   Both the Supreme Court and the National court have an inherent power to make, in such circumstances as seem to them proper, orders in the nature of prerogative writs and such other orders as are necessary to do justice in the circumstances of a particular case.

The Committee noted that there were two conflicting views on the issue. On the one hand, there was strong view advocated by many participants at the workshop that OLNLGE, section 220 being a constitutional law itself prohibits any appeal or review designed to question the decision of the National Court in any way. And that means the review jurisdiction in *Constitution*, section 155(2)(b) cannot be used to review a decision of the National Court in an election petition. This view was supported by experiences gained from the vast number of election petition reviews, from a wide range of decisions, from both interlocutory rulings and final decisions, filed by aggrieved parties under section 155(2)(b) and entertained by the Supreme Court. This was particularly so after the last (1997) national elections. As a result, there is a need to return to the letter of the law in OLNLGE, section 220 and stop the reviews altogether.

On the other hand, there is the prevailing view, in accordance with established precedent that OLNLGE, section 220 does not oust the inherent review jurisdiction of the Supreme Court conferred by *Constitution* section 155(2)(b). The principle was first developed in relation to criminal appeals in *Avia Aihi v The State* [1981] PNGLR 81 and later extended to election petition cases in *Balakau v Torato* [1983] PNGLR 242. In Balakau the Supreme court held that "Section 220 (OLNE) is constitutionally valid as it relates to the right of appeal, but is not purposed to prohibit the review power of this Court under section 155(2)(b) of the *Constitution*": Per Kidu CJ at p. 246. Prior to Balakau, it seems election petition reviews were unheard of. Balakau opened the door and consequently, following the 1987 Elections, there were a number of review applications filed and dealt with. And then following the 1992 Elections, there was an upsurge in election petition reviews. As a result, the National Court formulated the *Election Petition Practice Directions* to guide the conduct of election petition trials. These rules were reviewed in 1997 just before the 1997 Elections. After the 1997 Elections, the number of elections petitions filed and heard by the National Court reached all time high and this was followed by a floodgate of review applications filed before the Supreme Court and review upon review application filed under what is known as the 'slip-rule' principle.

In the absence of any rules on election petition reviews, the practice and procedure in relation to election petition reviews are as developed by the Supreme Court in cases on a case-by-case basis. Essentially, it has been decided that leave to apply for judicial review is not separately required for judicial review under section 155(2)(b), in relation to election petition cases: *SC Review 5 of 1998: Kasap v Yama* [1998 – 89] PNGLR 197; *Application by Mionzing* [1992] PNGLR 122; *Ivarato v. Lafanama* (1998), SC 563 and Application of *Ludwig Patrick Somare* (1998), SC 572. This means that an applicant for review is entitled to seek review of any ruling, interlocutory or final, almost as of right.

In relation to the substantive review, the criteria first developed in *Avia Aihi* and adopted and applied in Balakau and other subsequent cases are these:

(a) That it is in the interest of justice;
(b) That there are cogent and convincing reasons and exceptional circumstances where some substantial injustice is manifest or the case is of special gravity.
(c) There are clear legal grounds meriting a review of the decision.

These criteria were initially developed to guide the exercise of discretion under section 155(2)(b) in a criminal appeal where an applicant had lost his right to appeal. It seems that they have been adopted by the Supreme Court in election petition case where an applicant has no right of appeal and has lost none. It seems that the criteria have not been modified or tailored to make them appropriate to election petition reviews.

The broad nature of these criteria has led to the Supreme Court, constituted by different judges, making decisions which may appear at times inconsistent and encouraged a floodgate of review applications. The standard of scrutiny of the grounds for review under the above criteria may have varied from Court to Court resulting in more confusion. This has been more so in the election petition reviews filed after the 1997 Elections than in any other election.

The Committee explored both views extensively and resolved to recommend to the workshop as follows:

(a) The principles in Balakau may be revisited by the Supreme Court in an appropriate case. One way this could be facilitated is by a constitutional reference under section 18 or section 19 of the *Constitution*. One of the constitutional question that may be addressed is whether section 220 of the OLNLGE prohibits a review of the decision of the National Court under section 155(2)(b) of the *Constitution*, and if it does not, then what is the applicable criteria governing grant of review. Views already expressed or yet to be expressed by judges and participants at public forums may not necessarily be the view taken by judges in a proper judicial forum. Judges and participants attending the workshop are advised to be cautious with pressing their views on such issues as they may be prejudicial to the outcome of any constitutional challenge.

(b) By the same token, any suggestions made for reform of the present criteria for governing the grant of leave under section 155(2)(b) in limited cases should be addressed by judges of the Supreme Court in a proper judicial forum in an appropriate case.

2. Arguments in Favour of Restricting Review under Constitution Section 155(2)b

2.1 Until the Supreme Court re-visits the principles in Balakau the current practice will continue. The question then is how the present rules of practice developed by the Court in cases should be formulated in a coherent manner and improved to ensure that meritous applications are expeditiously disposed of in a fair manner.

2.2 The Committee is of the view that even though in principle, the criteria for the grant of judicial review laid down in the cases are restrictive in nature, the practical application of those criteria by the Court has been flexible and such that it has encouraged a floodgate of applications. Therefore, there is a need to further restrict the exercise of the review power in section 155(2)(b). Any rules formulated by the Court should reflect this need.

3. Rule Making Power of Judges of the Supreme Court

The Committee explored the rule making powers of the Supreme Court under the *Constitution* and the *Supreme Court Act*. The Committee was of the view that the judges of the Supreme Court may utilise their general rule-making power under section 184 of the *Constitution*, which clearly gives the Supreme Court judges power to make rules of Court under section 155(2)(b) of the *Constitution*. The invocation of this rule-making power in relation to judicial review cases brought under section 155(2)(b) of the *Constitution*, is not new. This power was invoked in formulating rules under the *Supreme Court Rules* 1984: see Order 5 of the *Supreme Court Rules* ('SCR') which provides a procedure for making an application under section

155(2)(b) of the *Constitution* for review of decision of the National Court.

4. Principles Underlying Election Petition Review Rule

Any rules formulated by the judges under section 184 of the *Constitution,* should be governed by sound underlying principles including:

(a) Respect for the proper function and role of the National Court as a quasi-judicial/statutory tribunal under the OLNLGE.
(b) Respect for the political process.
(c) Integrity of the decision-making process of the National Court and Supreme Court.
(d) Impartiality of decision making process of both the National Court and the Supreme Court.
(e) Fairness and firmness in decision-making.
(f) Transparency in the practice and procedure of both the National Court and the Supreme Court.
(g) Substantial justice based on clear legal merits of the case.
(h) Expedited hearing and prompt decision-making.
(i) Finality of decision of the National Court and the Supreme Court.
(j) Consistency in developing precedent.
(k) Being economical to all parties.

5. Supreme Court Election Review Rules

5.1 Order 5 of the *Supreme Court Rules* could be amended to add a new "Division 4" to provide for election reviews under section 155(2)(b), of a decision of the National Court made under OLNLGE, Part XVIII (Disputed Election Petition

Returns, etc). Once the rules are made by the judges, they take immediate effect. They are required to be tabled in Parliament by the Chief Justice but the tabling of the Rules in Parliament is not a pre-condition to the coming into operation of the rules. And if the Parliament were to consider the rules or some of it were to be either inconsistent with the OLNLGE or a subject matter for the Legislature, the Parliament could disallow them.

5.2 Contents of New Review Rules

The proceeding part of this paper sets out the *Supreme Court Election Review Rules* followed by commentaries. As there are no model review rules to guide the committee, the committee resorted to relevant rules of the Supreme Court and the *National Court Rules* governing ordinary judicial reviews and appeals.

"Division 4: REVIEW UNDER SECTION 155(2)(b) OF THE CONSTITUTION OF NATIONAL COURT DECISION MADE UNDER PART XVIII OF OLNLGE

Commentary: This is the proposed title to the new division. A more detailed heading is necessary to differentiate between other ordinary types of reviews covered by Order 5.

Sub-division 1—Application for Leave to apply for Review.

1. *An application for review of a decision made by the National Court under part XVIII of the OLNLGE made under section 155(2)(b) of the Constitution shall be filed under this division.*

Commentary: This is a general jurisdiction provision.

2. *An application under s.155(2)(b) in respect of a decision of the National Court under Part XVIII of the OLNLGE lies to the court only with leave.*

Commentary: The requirement for leave is a standard requirement for the review of decisions of quasi-judicial or statutory tribunals. Although the Supreme Court has treated a court of Disputed Returns described in the OLNLGE, as the same as a National Court, the true nature of the process set out in the OLNLGE is quasi-judicial, because the National Court is not required to apply technical rules of practice and procedure and evidence. Also, the decision is not subject to appeal by an aggrieved party through the normal appeal process, as of right. Therefore, the grant of leave is a prerequisite to a review, which must be applied for and obtained separately.

3. *An application for review shall not be made in respect of an interlocutory ruling, judgement or order until after the hearing of the petition.*

Commentary: This provision is consistent with changes in rule 10(c). All interlocutory orders and substantive issues raised (together with rule 13 of the *National Court Election Petition Rules*) during the trial by the same judge and a single decision made on all issues raised at the hearing will be dealt with. If any interlocutory applications are entertained by chance and rulings made before the hearing of the substantive issues, then any review of such decision will not be allowed, until after the completion of the substantive hearing. As to what is an interlocutory judgement and a final judgement see *Ruma Construction Pty Ltd v Christopher Smith* SC600 (1999) and *NCDC v Namo Trading Pty Ltd* SC663 (2001).

4. *An application for leave shall be made by:*

   (a) application ex-parte to a single judge of the Supreme Court; and

   (b) shall be in form 5A and shall:

      (i) be entitled under section 155(2)(b) of the Constitution, together with the year and maker of the application;

      (ii) be entitled in the name of the person making the application;

      (iii) state briefly the particulars of the judicial act to be reviewed;

      (iv) state the grounds upon which the review is sought;

      (v) the order sought in lieu thereof;

      (vi) be signed by the person seeking the review and not by his lawyer or anyone else; and

      (vii) be filed in the Registry at Waigani.

Commentary: These formal requirements are adopted from SCR Order 5 rule 1 except for (iv), which we consider is necessary. This requirement is similar to an application for leave to appeal where the grounds of the application are required to be particularised. The application is to be heard by a single judge of the Supreme Court (see similar provision in section 10(1) and section 17 of the *Supreme Court Act* in relation to application for leave to appeal).

The traditional position at common law which is reflected in NCR Order 16 rule 3(1) is that an application for leave for judicial review is made strictly ex parte.

This requirement is subject of some controversy among judges. Some judges strictly apply Order 16 rule 3(1) and conduct *ex parte* hearing whereas other judges have taken a liberal view and allowed leave application to proceed inter-parties: see Amet CJ and Hinchliffe J in *Ombudsman*

Commission v. Donohoe [1990] PNGLR 153 and Hinchliffe J. in *Manjin v PTC* [1990] PNGLR 288 who favoured the former view and for the latter view, see Sheehan J. in *Ombudsman Commission v. Donohoe,* supra. Sheehan J's view has been criticised as *"novel, as it is unfounded"*: see Michael M. Ntumy; *Leave Applications For Judicial Review* (Port Moresby: UPNG Press, 1996) 43.

The Committee endorses the views expressed by Amet CJ and Hinchliffe, J. because if leave applications were allowed to be made inter-parties, the judge will most likely be bogged down with complex and lengthy arguments on procedure, facts and law which will defeat the purpose of achieving an expedited determination on what is otherwise a preliminary point.

The requirement that an applicant himself or herself sign the application for leave is consistent with the judicial review.

The Registrar is requested to draft an appropriate form 5A for approval by the judges.

5. *No respondent shall be heard in an application made under Rule 4.*

Commentary: See commentary in Rule 4, *supra*. This rule emphasises the significance of an ex parte hearing.

6. *The application for leave must be filed within 7 days of the decision sought to be reviewed or until such time as extended by a judge, upon application, made within 7 days.*

Commentary: Placing time limits is an essential pre-requisite for ordinary judicial review applications. The time limit allowed under NCR, Order 16 rule 4(2) is 4 months. We believe this period is too long. A shorter time frame of 7 days is appropriate. Also see section 17 of the *Supreme Court Act* which requires application for extension of time to appeal being filed within the period prescribed for filing an appeal.

7. *The application for leave shall be supported by:*

   (a) a statement signed by the applicant setting out the name and description of the applicant, the background circumstances pertaining to the application, the relief sought, the grounds on which the relief is sought; and
   (b) an affidavit of the applicant verifying the facts relied on;
   (c) have annexed:
      (i) a copy of the petition;
      (ii) written judgement of the National Court, if any, or a transcribed copy of the judgment;
      (iii) any written submissions of the parties before the National Court;
      (iv) any other material the applicant considers relevant for the application for leave.

Commentary: The requirements in (a) and (b) are similar to NCR, Order 16 rule 3(2). We consider the documents enumerated in 7(c) above are necessary for purpose of determining the leave application. In relation to (c)(ii), we consider that the delivery of a written judgment by the National Court is preferable, but if that were not possible, a transcribed copy of the oral judgment delivered should be made available to the parties immediately. By requiring the applicant to file these documents, it is intended to place a heavy onus on the applicant to demonstrate to the Court, on the face of the originating process documentation, that the applicant has a case worthy of judicial intervention by way of review. The requirement in (c) is similar to SCR Order 10 rule 3.

8. *The applicant shall serve the documents filed under rules 4 and 7 above, on the Attorney General and the Electoral Commission not later than 2 days before the application is made.*

Commentary: This requirement is similar to NCR, Order 16 rule 3(b)(3) in respect to service on the Attorney General. Service on the Electoral Commission is a new procedure but it is intended to give the Electoral Commission, the government body directly responsible for electoral matters, early notice of the application.

9. *The Registrar shall fix a date for the hearing of the application for leave within 14 days from the date of filing the application for leave unless a judge orders otherwise.*

Commentary: Under NCR, no time limit is fixed for the hearing of the leave application. As time is of essence in elections, we consider that a time period prescribed for the hearing of the leave application is appropriate.

10. *Leave shall not be granted unless the judge is satisfied that:*

   a. *The applicant has sufficient interest in the matter to which the application relates; and*
   b. *The applicant has a serious issue to be argued at the hearing of the substantive application, with respect to the following matters:*

      (i) *It is in the interest of justice; and*
      (ii) *There are cogent and convincing reasons and exceptional circumstances; and*
      (iii) *These are clear legal grounds meriting a review of the decision; and*

c. *The application is not frivolous, vexatious, or an abuse of the process of the court.*

Commentary: The opening sentence of this rule is couched in the negative to reflect the view that leave is not available as a matter of course but only in limited cases and is restricted to cases which have clear legal merit, which are pertinent to recognised grounds of review.

Rule 10(a) is general criteria as to *locus standi* of the applicant in leave applications: see NCR, Order 16 rule 3(5). Ordinarily, it will be restricted to a person who is a party to the election petition proceedings in the National Court and who is aggrieved by that decision.

Rule 10(b) departs from the criteria or test in ordinary judicial review leave applications or in leave to appeal applications in ordinary appeals where the "arguable case", test is applied. This reflects the principle that judicial review is granted only in cases where there are cogent and convincing reasons and exceptional circumstances and there are clear legal grounds meriting a review. Rule 10(b) then requires the issues to be relevant to the proposed grounds upon which an application for review is granted. These are the same criteria established in *Avia Aihi* adopted in the *Balakau* case and other subsequent cases.

Rule 10(c) introduces additional criteria where the proposed grounds of review are subjected to strict scrutiny to ensure that only applications with clear legal merit proceed to a substantive review. This criteria is important because election petition cases are particularly emotive and permeated by political considerations and are more likely than not to attract frivolous and vexations applications and which abuse the court review process.

The criteria in Rule 10(a), (b) and (c) are conjunctive. This is shown by the use of the word "and" as opposed to "or". That is, an applicant must satisfy all 3 criteria. The criteria in (b)(i)(ii) and (iii) are also conjunctive. The case authorities may suggest that the Court may grant or refuse to grant a review on any one of these criteria, (see *Yama v Gubag* SC 547(1998)) but we, suggest that these criteria should go together.

11. *A decision to grant or refusal to grant leave is final and shall not be appealed against or questioned in any way.*

Commentary: This rule prevents any appeal from a decision to grant or refusal to grant leave. In appeals against a decision under NCR Order 16, an order granting or refusing to grant leave may be appealed against (see SCR Order 10 and NCR Order 16 rule 11). This rule departs from that practice. If an appeal were allowed, the whole review process would become protracted, time consuming and the purpose of OLNLGE, section 220 defeated.

This practice also departs from the practice in an ordinary appeal where a decision of a single judge of the Supreme Court refusing an application for leave to appeal, may be followed by a fresh application before a full bench of the Supreme Court: (see section 10(2) of the *Supreme Court Act).*

Subdivision 2—Application for Review

12. *Within 7 days of grant of leave, an application for review shall be filed in Form 5B.*

Commentary: It is considered that 7 days is adequate time for the applicant to prepare and file the substantive review application (see NCR, Order 16 r 5). The Registrar will devise Form 5B. This form is similar to SCR Form 5. This form shall state the name of the applicant seeking review, the judicial act to be reviewed, and where appropriate state the order of the National Court and annex a copy of that order; a statement that leave was granted by a judge; the grounds upon which leave to apply for judicial review was granted, and the order or relief sought. This form must be signed by the person seeking review and not by his lawyer or any other person.

13. *At the time of filing the application for review under rule 12, the applicant shall deposit with the Registrar of the Supreme Court the sum of K5,000.00 as security for costs into the Registrar's Trust Account.*

Commentary: OLNLGE section 209 requires a deposit of K2,500.00 for security for costs to cover costs of proceeding before the National Court. This amount is not intended to cover costs on review, which are expected to be higher. There should be a separate security for costs on review.

The amount for security for costs on review should be doubled. The applicant, who is granted leave to apply for judicial review, must make this deposit to cover the costs on review.

14. *Within 21 days of the grant of leave, the applicant shall serve the Application for Review, and copies of documents filed under rules 4 and 7 on the respondents named in the application and on any other person the Court considers has a direct interest in the application.*

Commentary: Service of the application on parties directly affected by the application who are normally the respondents to the application. This is a standard requirement in review application (see NCR, Order 16 rule 5(2). It also leaves room for the Court to direct service of the documents on any person who might have a direct interest in the application but not named by the applicant as a party to the proceedings, e.g. a losing candidate in the election in question who might benefit from the review.

A greater period of 21 days is allowed to enable the applicant to effect service on the respondent, particularly respondents other than the Electoral Commission, who may be difficult to locate.

15. *Within 30 days of the grant of leave, the applicant shall:*
    (a) *file a draft Index to the Review Book;*
    (b) *obtain a date from the Registrar to settle the Index; and*
    (c) *serve the index on the respondent together with a Notice of Appointment for the settlement of the Index to the Review Book.*

Commentary: This rule is similar to the rules governing settlement of Index to Appeal Book (see SCR Order 7 rule 33–41).

16. *The Registrar shall settle the Index to the Review Book at the date appointed for the settlement and shall:*

    (a) *determine what documents and matters shall be included in the appeal book and the order of inclusion and such other matters as he thinks fit concerning the preparation of copies of the appeal papers;*
    (b) *settle the index in accordance with Rule 17 sub-rule (l);*
    (c) *determine the number of copies of the appeal book required;*

17. *The Review Book in Relation to Election Petition Review.*

    (a) *The review book for use of the hearing of a review shall be prepared in bound volumes or a suitable binder on paper of such size.*
    (b) *The thickness of any one volume of the review book shall not exceed 38mm.*

(c) *The title pages shall give the full and correct title of the proceedings, and the names of the lawyers for each party (if any), telephone numbers and their addresses for service.*

(d) *After the title page there shall follow the index consisting of a complete list of the documents contained in the review book as settled by the Registrar, stating in the case of each document indicating at what page of the review book it appears.*

(e) *In the Index, the exhibits shall be arranged in the order in which they have been lettered or numbered in the National Court sittings as Court of Disputed Returns.*

(f) *The date and a short description of each document shall precede it, but backsheet or formal heading shall not be printed or copied, and jurats, format identification of exhibits and the like shall be omitted.*

(g) *Where the transcript of evidence is reproduced, the name of the witness together with a notation indicating whether the evidence given is in chief (IC), cross examination (XX) or re-examination (RX) shall appear on the right hand side of each page.*

(h) *A copy of the review book shall be examined with the original documents, and all copies shall be corrected.*

(i) *The examined copy of the review book shall be filed in the Registry with a certificate by the parties or their lawyers that it has been examined and is correct.*

(j) *The review book shall be prepared and produced in a manner satisfactory to the Registrar.*

(k) *Only such documents as are relevant or necessary shall be included in the review book.*

(l) *The review papers shall be paginated and the documents arranged in the following order:*

1. *The Application for Review to the Supreme Court;*
2. *Process for review;*

3. *Evidence, oral or affidavit, stating the name of each witness or deponent and page number on which such evidence commences;*
4. *Testimony taken on commission or before an examiner and put in or used as evidence;*
5. *Exhibits arranged in the order in which they have been lettered or numbers as exhibits in the National Court;*
6. *The reasons for judgement or orders of the primary judge or Court;*
7. *The formal judgements or orders of the primary Judge or Court;*
8. *The certificate that the review book has been examined and is correct.*

18. *Unless the Court otherwise orders, the applicant shall not less than 7 days before the commencement of the hearing:*
    (a) file with the Registrar; and
    (b) serve on the respondents separately represented, copies of the Review Book.

Commentary: SCR, Order 7 rule 44 adopted with appropriate modifications.

19. *The Registrar shall set down the review for hearing within 30 days from the grant of leave, and notice of such hearing shall be immediately served on the respondent by the applicant in accordance with form 5C.*

Commentary: SCR Order 7 rule 47 – 48 adopted with appropriate modifications. The idea is that within a time frame of 30 days from the grant of leave, an applicant shall complete all steps necessary to get the review ready for a hearing, on the date fixed for hearing. The Registrar is requested to formulate an appropriate form 5C.

20. *Any time limit prescribed by rules 12, 14, 15, 16 and 18 may be extended by a judge on application made within the time prescribed by that rule.*

Commentary: This rule gives flexibility to the Court and the parties to obtain an extension of time, where practical difficulties hinder the parties from complying with the rules in time. e.g. delay in obtaining transcript of proceedings, copies of orders or judgments from the Registry; difficulty in effecting service of documents, etc.

Given the need to strictly comply with time limits, the grant of an extension will be more of an exception than the general rule. An extension should not be granted except where good grounds are shown by an applicant.

Sub-Division 3: Hearing of Application for Review

21. Evidence which were not before the National Court shall not be allowed at the hearing unless the Court upon application or on its own motion, otherwise orders.

Commentary: Similar to SCR, Order 7 rule 57. This rule prevents a party from introducing fresh evidence at the hearing. Judicial Review is about reviewing the procedure and decision reached by the tribunal as evident on the face of the record. As a general rule all parties should be confined to the materials that was placed before the National Court as contained in the record of proceedings.

22. *Once an application for review is fixed for hearing, the Court shall not adjourn the hearing unless there are exceptional circumstances.*

Commentary: Similar to Order 7 rule 66 of the *Supreme Court Rules*: see *Kidu v Karo* (Unpublished decision of the

Supreme Court in SCA No. 46 of 1998) dated 5 June 1998, cited in *Yasona v Maibawa* SC (1998) 589. These cases emphasise the point that time is of essence and cases listed for hearing must proceed on the day fixed unless special circumstances exist.

23. *An application for review shall not be granted by the Court except where:*

    (a) It is in the interest of justice; and
    (b) That there are cogent and convincing reasons and exceptional circumstances where some substantial injustice is manifest or the case is of special gravity; and
    (c) There are clear legal grounds meriting a review of the decision.

Commentary: These are the same criteria laid down and explained by the Supreme Court governing the grant of review in many cases. The same commentary in relation to use of the word "and" in rule 10 applies here.

24. *The court may grant any of the following relief, including:*

    a. An order in the nature of pre-rogative writs; and
    b. Any such other orders as are necessary to do justice in the circumstances of a particular case but it shall not make any orders, which the National Court is not empowered to make under Part XVIII of the OLNLGE.

Commentary: Rule 24(a) spells out the relief that the Supreme Court may grant in review (see NCR, Order 16 rule 1). These reliefs are available in an ordinary review. *Constitution,* s.155(4) also allows for pre-rogative writs.

Rule 24(b) provides additional relief provided for in s.155(4) of the *Constitution.*

The latter proviso is intended to ensure that any relief or order that the Supreme Court makes is a relief that the National Court had jurisdiction to make under the OLNLGE. This is because the relief available to the National Court hearing an election petition is prescribed by the OLNLGE.

25. *The Court may direct that multiple applications in relation to the one election or return be consolidated for the purpose of the hearing.*

Commentary: This rule departs from the current practice in that it forces parties to consolidate multiple reviews: see *Iangalio v Ranyeta & Electoral Commission*, (1998) SC 568 in relation to an election petition before the National Court. Also see *Tulapi v Luta & Basua*, (2001) SC 653. It is undesirable to conduct separate reviews in relation to the one and same election or return because different reviews before differently constituted Courts may produce different results, which may be inconsistent or contradictory.

26. *Where an applicant has not done any act required to be done by or under these rules or otherwise have not prosecuted his application with due diligence, the court may:*

    (a) *order that the review be dismissed for want of prosecution; or*
    (b) *fix a time pre-emptorarily for the doing of the act and order that upon non-compliance, the review should stand dismissed for want of prosecution; or*
    (c) *may make any Order that it deems just.*

Commentary: SCR, Order 7 rule 53 adopted with appropriate modification.

27. *The Respondent may make an application for an Order under Rule 26 and the Court may after notice has been given to the Applicant by the Respondent or the Registrar, make such orders.*

Sub-Division 4: Court May Give Directions

28. *Where an application has been filed, the Court may give such directions as may be required including the terms of the reviews, the matters to be included in it and provision of lawyers or parties for the argument of it.*

Commentary: See similar provision in SCR, Order 9 rule 5. This provision allows the Court the flexibility to issue directions as to the conduct of the review at any stage of the proceedings.

Sub-Division 5: Stay of enforcement of decision sought to be reviewed

29. *No application shall be made to stay the effect or enforcement of the decision of the National Court voiding an election or return which is sought to be reviewed.*

Commentary: A decision of the National Court is final and self-executing; a stay order is not available: In *Sauk v Poliye,* (2000) SC 618. In that case, the Supreme Court dealt with an application by Mr. Sauk whose election was declared void and a by-election was ordered. He filed an application for review. He then applied to stay the order voiding his election so that he could remain a Member of Parliament and continue to be a Minister of the government, pending the hearing of his application for review. He did not apply to stay the order for a by-election. The Supreme Court refused the application.

In *Fr. Ambane v Sumeno & Anor,* Unpublished Supreme Court Judgment in SCRev. 61//98 of Amet CJ, Salika, J and Sevua J, dated 3/6/98, a case which was not cited by counsel in *Sauk's* case, the Court was of the same view. But in that case, whilst the decision voiding the election and removing Fr. Ambane from continuing to be a Member of the Parliament pending the determination of his review application was not stayed, the decision ordering a by-election was stayed because to allow a by-election to proceed whilst the review was pending would defeat the purpose of the review.

Sub-Division 6: Costs

30. *The Court may make such orders as to costs as it deems fit.*

Commentary: This rule is not new and it requires no explanation. It appears there is no Supreme Court rules on costs. The practice is that costs are taxed under the NCR. The Registrar or Taxing Officer will be invited to comment on the current practice. As to principles on costs on review, see *Maino v Avei,* (2000) SC 633.

5.3 Final Comments on the Rules

A distinction is maintained between "a judge" and "the Court". The former refers to a single judge of the Supreme Court and the latter to the full bench of the Supreme Court. It is intended that a single judge will deal with pre-hearing matters including leave applications and the Court will deal with the substantive hearings and matters arising therefrom.

It is intended that all preliminary/interlocutory matters, (including leave applications) will be completed within 30 days from the grant of leave and 40 days from the decision of the National Court. It is hoped that the substantive hearing will take place as soon as practicable, say within 2-3 months from the date of grant of leave.

As to whether the time limits are sufficient to do the things required by the rules, such as for instance, provision of Court transcripts, is a matter that Mr. Dean Henderson (Consultant – Court Reporting Section) and Mr. Laurence Newell (Registrar of Courts) have both made comments and their comments have been considered and incorporated into the revised draft Rules.

These rules do not make provision for application under the "Slip–Rule" principle. As to whether or not the rules should make provision for "slip-rule" applications is an issue that is open for discussion. The Committee did not express any views but simply raised the issue for discussion.

SUPREME COURT ELECTION PETITION REVIEW FORMS

Supreme Court Election Review Form 5A

Application for Leave to Review Under Section 155 (2)
(b) of the Constitution

In the Supreme Court of Justice — SC Review No of 20

A.B.
Applicant/

APPLICATION will be made to a single Judge at the Supreme Court, Waigani (or at ....) at ... am on the ... day of ... 200... For Leave to Review
(Particulars of the Judicial Act to be reviewed)

Grounds upon which the review is sought: (state grounds on which application is based)

Order sought in lieu thereof:

Dated:
Sgd___________________
(Applicant in person)

FILED at the Supreme Court Registry in Waigani

BY:

Name (Personal)	Name (Lawyer)
Address	Address
(postal and e-mail where available)	(postal and e-mail where available)
Telephone	Telephone
Fax	Fax

Supreme Court Election Review Form 5B

Form of Application to Review Election Proceedings under Constitutions 155(2)(6)

In the Supreme Court of Justice — S.C. REV. NO. ... of 200 ... (Insert number and year)

Review Pursuant to Constitution Section 155(2)(b)

Application by (insert name of person seeking Review)

Leave having been given by Justice … …on… …at… …

1. This Review of the National Court is sought by (insert name of person seeking the review).
2. The Judicial Acto to be Reviewed is:
   National Court No:
   Parties:
   Date of Order:
   Order:
   (Where appropriate, a copy of the National Court Order is to be stated and annexed).
3. Grounds (specify each particular ground by paragraph where leave has been granted)
4. Order (state relief sought).

Dated:

Sgd__________________
(To be signed by person seeking the review)
Filed at the Supreme Court Registry in Waigani

By:

Name (Personal)	Name (Lawyer)
Address	Address
(postal and e-mail where available)	(postal and e-mail where available)
Telephone	Telephone
Fax	Fax

Supreme Court Election Review Form 5C

General Form of Notice of Hearing Notice

This (state proceedings) will be heard at the sittings of the Supreme Court, Waigani, (or such other place as specified), commencing on the day of ...

Further details can be obtained from the Registry.

Signed ____________________
Registrar

Signed ____________________
Applicant (in person) or Representative

FILED at the Supreme Court Registry at Waigani

BY:

Name (Personal)	Name (Lawyer)
Address	Address
(postal and e-mail where available)	(postal and e-mail where available)
Telephone	Telephone
Fax	Fax

INDEX